Key Terms in Philosophy of Religion

Continuum *Key Terms in Philosophy*

The *Key Terms* series offers undergraduate students clear, concise and accessible introductions to core topics. Each book includes a comprehensive overview of the key terms, concepts, thinkers and texts in the area covered and ends with a guide to further resources.

Available now:

Key Terms in Logic, edited by Jon Williamson and Federica Russo
Key Terms in Philosophy of Mind, Pete Mandik

***Key Terms in Philosophy* forthcoming from Continuum:**

Aesthetics, Brent Kalar
Ethics, Oskari Kuusela
Political Philosophy, Jethro Butler

Key Terms in Philosophy of Religion

Raymond J. VanArragon

continuum

Continuum International Publishing Group

The Tower Building
11 York Road
London SE1 7NX

80 Maiden Lane
Suite 704
New York, NY 10038

www.continuumbooks.com

British Library Cataloguing-in-Publication Data
A catalogue record for this book is available from the British Library.

ISBN: HB: 978-1-4411-6013-3
     PB: 978-1-4411-3867-5

Library of Congress Cataloging-in-Publication Data
VanArragon, Raymond J.
  Key terms in philosophy of religion / Raymond VanArragon.
    p. cm.
  Includes bibliographical references and index.
  ISBN: 978-1-4411-6013-3
  ISBN: 978-1-4411-3867-5 (pb)
  1. Religion–Philosophy–Textbooks. 2. Religion–Philosophy–Terminology.
  I. Title.
  BL51.V335 2010
  210.3–dc22

                 2010005481

Typeset by Newgen Imaging Systems Pvt Ltd, Chennai, India
Printed and bound in Great Britain by the MPG Books Group

Contents

Acknowledgments

My thanks to those philosophers who have taught me most about philosophy of religion, particularly Kelly James Clark, C. Stephen Evans, Alvin Plantinga, and Eleonore Stump. Thanks to William Ramsey, one of the best philosophy teachers I have ever come across, whose even-handedness and clarity of expression I have always sought to emulate. Thanks also to the many people who have helped me with this book by reading and evaluating entries: Derek Pierson, Matthew Schellenberg, Gary and Gretchen VanArragon, Joseph Vukov, my colleagues in the Philosophy Department at Bethel University, and especially my wife, Janel VanArragon. This book is dedicated to her and to our children, Caleb and Kathryn.

Preface: How to Read This Book

This book is organized as follows. The first chapter provides an introduction to our subject by briefly exploring the nature of religion, the relation of philosophy to religion (of reason to faith), the main topics in philosophy of religion, and the methods of philosophy. The second chapter, by far the longest in the book, covers key terms in philosophy of religion, while the third and fourth chapters cover key thinkers and key texts. Here are four points to guide you as you read.

First, in the second chapter terms are listed alphabetically, with explanations of various lengths following each term. In the explanation of one term I often mention other terms (and thinkers and texts) covered elsewhere in the book. The first time one term is used in the explanation of another, that term is in bold print. If you see a bold-printed term in an explanation, you can infer that that term (or thinker, or text) has its own entry elsewhere in the book. (Sometimes a variation on a term is in bold, as when "omnipotent" is highlighted even though "omnipotence" is the term with the entry.) In general, my goal has been to make each term's explanation self-standing, so that the reader should be able to gain a good understanding of that term by reading the discussion that follows it, and without needing to flip through the book in order to understand the terms used in the explanation of the original term. Still, the explanations of bold-print terms, in the context of an entry for a different term, are bound to be cursory. Readers are encouraged to deepen their understanding by turning to entries for related terms as they see fit.

Second, entries are intended to introduce readers to the concepts and debates, rather than give anything like a final word on them. For that reason, suggestions for further reading are included at the end of many entries, particularly those which leave off without resolution or where questions are indicated without being explored. Some of these readings can be found reprinted in different philosophy of religion anthologies currently on the market.

Third, entries in the third and fourth chapters are organized similarly to those in the second chapter, but are not necessarily self-standing. Full understanding of a thinker's contributions or the main issues in a text may require readers to flip back to terms in the previous chapter. (As before, terms, thinkers, and texts which are covered elsewhere in the book are listed in bold print the first time they come up in an entry.) Thus these chapters are largely intended to piggy-back on the second chapter—a strategy that helps the reader to connect thinkers and texts with terms and concepts, and also prevents needless repetition.

Finally, the book has a fairly thorough index. If you are curious about some concept from philosophy of religion that you don't find listed in the second chapter of the book, it may be that it is in fact discussed but doesn't have its own entry. In that case, it should be referenced in the index. (For terms, thinkers, and texts that do have their own entries, the entries' page numbers are in bold type.) Note also that the index includes names of authors whose writings are recommended for further reading after entries in the second chapter, but are not explicitly discussed.

My hope is that this book will be a useful resource for anyone interested in these topics. And who wouldn't find these topics interesting! Religion is of central importance in the lives of many people, and it represents a force to be reckoned with even for those who aren't especially enamored of it. It seems essential, then, to subject religion to philosophical scrutiny, to analyze religious belief in general, its justification and legitimacy, the reasons for and against it, and to investigate some of the specific claims that particular religious traditions tend to make. Fortunately for us, work on these topics has been of particularly high quality in the last few decades, drawing on new insights and extending the debates from centuries past. I hope this book helps to draw you into the discussion.

Introduction to Philosophy of Religion

Philosophy of religion is the area of philosophy that takes philosophical methods and applies them to matters of religious concern. In other words, it applies reason to faith. The results of this application—and the mere fact that it is made—are both fascinating and the source of enormous controversy. In this chapter we'll look briefly at what religion is, at different approaches to the application of philosophy to religion, at the topics that philosophy of religion typically focuses on, and at some basics of philosophical reasoning.

Nature of religion

Religion is a phenomenon with which we're all familiar. It typically involves acknowledgment of a divine reality and the requirement of obedience to it; it includes rites and ceremonies that mark the human relation to this reality; and it has enormous impact on the way that its adherents see the world and their place in it. There are a number of different world religions with millions and even billions of followers. The different religions make unique claims about the divine reality and also claim special access to it, either by way of direct revelation from the reality itself or through the witness of individuals who were or are especially attuned to it.

So, different religions with their different traditions and histories make claims about the divine reality that their adherents buy into. But what is the nature of these claims? In answering this question, we can begin to see why there might be tension between the methods of philosophy and the content of religion—a tension between reason and faith. Religious traditions often make claims that cannot be verified in scientific ways and which are in an important sense removed from our ordinary experience. Consider the following sample. The major theistic religions (Christianity, Islam, and Judaism) claim that there exists a God, a great invisible being who created everything and who is all-powerful, all-knowing, and perfectly good; but of course we cannot *see* such a being, and millions of people believe there is no such thing.

Some of the great Eastern religions, including Buddhism and Hinduism, accept a doctrine of reincarnation which claims that after death people are born again as other people (or perhaps other creatures), a process that is repeated until some kind of enlightened goal is achieved. This doctrine seems difficult to prove. Christians believe that God is a trinity, one God but three persons, one of whom became human and whose death and subsequent resurrection made possible human salvation; Muslims believe that the Angel Gabriel appeared in visions to the prophet Muhammad; Jews and Christians believe that thousands of years ago God chose the people of Israel and led them from Egypt to the Promised Land, parting the Red Sea and destroying the Egyptian army in the process. These again are all eye-opening claims, and it seems profoundly difficult to verify any of them by the methods commonly used in other great truth-seeking enterprises such as science and mathematics. In any case, they aren't typically believed on the basis of such verification; instead, they are understood by adherents to the religions as being somehow divinely revealed.

Thus faith beliefs seem to be of a different order from what we could call reason beliefs, the paradigmatic examples of which include beliefs based on observation and rational reflection, beliefs in the sciences and in mathematics. This difference can lead to trouble when faith beliefs conflict (or appear to conflict) with reason beliefs. It can also lead to trouble when the faith beliefs of one tradition conflict with those of another, or, worse, when one tradition calls for violence against followers of another. When religious groups are convinced that their claims are divinely inspired, it is not easy to resolve such disagreements through rational discussion. The history of religion is fraught with examples of conflict that appear to stem in part from the very nature of religious faith.

Religion and philosophy

So, how should we think about these eye-opening religious claims, about the grounds for believing them and about the disagreements that result from them? In asking this question, we are already straying into philosophy, a discipline that employs rational methods of argument and analysis to try to understand the world we live in. Some religious believers, however, do not want to stray any farther than this: they think it altogether improper to subject their religious beliefs to any sort of philosophical scrutiny. These beliefs, after all, are divinely revealed, so to question them would be to doubt their source, and to analyze them would be futile since human reason cannot comprehend the divine. They must simply be believed. Such believers, in holding this position, endorse an extreme version of what is called *fideism*, which proclaims that reason and faith don't mix, because philosophy has no role to play in supporting or evaluating religious claims.

On the other side are those who believe that philosophy (and the sciences) should be brought to bear on religion, but should do so by ruling out religious faith altogether. These champions of reason endorse an extreme version of what can be called *rationalism*. We are rational beings, and we cannot set that fact aside in matters of religion. We cannot depend on so-called divine revelation, since beliefs attributed to it are really nothing more than poisonous superstition. We must instead depend on reason, which employs observation and logical principles in order to arrive at the truth. Again, reason and faith—philosophy and religion—don't mix, this time because the former leaves no room for the latter.

These positions, extreme fideism and extreme rationalism, express the outer edges between which philosophy of religion these days is done. Most philosophers take more moderate positions than these on the relation between faith and reason. Toward the fideism side, there are philosophers who acknowledge that religious faith includes claims which reason cannot prove are true (or even fully comprehend), but who nonetheless hold that if reason can demonstrate that those beliefs are not only mysterious but also false, then those faith beliefs should be abandoned. In other words, on this view faith beliefs have autonomy and authority but can nonetheless be checked by reason. Toward the rationalism side, there are philosophers who agree that religious beliefs must be positively supported by evidence, but argue against extreme rationalists that some of them *can* be supported in that way. These philosophers caution, however, that the demand for evidence should not be applied more harshly to religious beliefs than to other kinds of beliefs, and that evidence can be good evidence even if not everyone is convinced by it. (We often accept political or philosophical beliefs on the basis of reasons that don't convince everyone; but we still consider those beliefs to be rationally acceptable.) In this way, religious believers and non-believers search out the truth in philosophy of religion with differing inclinations about the role of reason and the legitimacy of faith.

Topics in philosophy of religion

The topics covered in philosophy of religion are many, but perhaps can helpfully be divided into three categories. First, there are the epistemological questions which constitute some of the background to the discipline. What is required for rational or justified belief? What is required for knowledge? Must a belief be based on evidence in order for it to be rational, justified, or known? The answers to these questions can be applied to *all* beliefs, of course; but they can also be applied to religious belief, and in recent years the application has been made in groundbreaking ways. Questions about the requirements for rational or justified religious belief really bring us back to the issues just discussed about the relation between faith and reason; and hence they are central questions in philosophy of religion.

Second, there are philosophical questions about religion in general. In this category we study the nature of religious language and religious experience. For the former, can our concepts apply to the divine? Are our conceptions of the divine affected by cultural factors or influenced by harmful prejudices? For the latter, what makes an experience religious? Are such experiences common from religion to religion? This question leads to a further question about religion in general: How should we think about the phenomenon of religious diversity? Do the different religions represent legitimate paths to the same end, or are differences between them more fundamental than that?

A third category of topics in philosophy of religion involves subjecting specific religious claims to philosophical scrutiny, by giving arguments for and against them as well as exploring their meanings and implications. Much work in this category relates to beliefs about God, as philosophers provide arguments for and against God's existence and ponder what God is like and what implications the divine nature has for morality and for human free will. Philosophical questions are raised about many other religious claims as well, including belief in miracles and human immortality.

These three categories (which can overlap with each other) give us a way to understand the topics in philosophy of religion. This book covers terms and concepts that fall into these categories, with special emphasis on the question of whether evidence is required for justified religious belief, on the issue of religious diversity, on arguments for and against God's existence (including the problem of evil), and on particular beliefs about God's nature and God's action and influence in the world.

Philosophical arguments

Thus far in this chapter, we have discussed the nature of religion and the claims that religious traditions tend to make, the relation between philosophy and religion, and the kinds of topics we encounter in philosophy of religion. Here we need to say something briefly about the way philosophy is done, and in particular the way philosophers attempt to establish conclusions. They do this by using *arguments*, and since a good deal of what's to come will involve explaining arguments connected with religious belief, we should pause here a moment to consider what arguments are.

An argument in philosophy is simply a set of statements, called *premises*, put forward in support of a conclusion. Philosophers deal in arguments all of the time, and this is not a bad thing. Philosophical arguments do not need to involve calling people names, throwing things, or storming off in a huff. Instead, it is with arguments that we try to persuade people that a particular claim is true or false. Arguments are an essential part of any rational debate.

As you read philosophy books (or encounter any other attempts to persuade you of something), you are likely to come across arguments for conclusions that you're not really sure about. What can you do then? If you ponder an argument, grasp its premises and see the way that they together support the conclusion, and if the argument seems to you to be absolutely solid and above reproach, then you have good reason to accept the conclusion. But not all arguments are that compelling. If you find the conclusion dubious and wish to question the argument, there are two things you might do. First, you might question whether the premises are true. If you suspect that a premise is false, or you don't think that you have very good reason for believing that it's true, then you might for the moment maintain your doubts about the argument and the conclusion it yields. Second, you might ask as you evaluate an argument whether the premises really do support the conclusion. Perhaps the inference is in fact a shaky one, so that even if the premises are true, they don't really provide good reason for believing the conclusion. If so, again, you should probably reject the argument and wait to see if a better one can be produced.

Two simple examples can illustrate the basics of this approach to arguments. Suppose someone claims that the American moon landing in 1969 was staged (it was filmed in the Arizona desert), and argues for this claim as follows. The flag the astronauts planted waved as if in the wind; a flag could only wave that way if there really were a wind; there was no wind on the moon; therefore, that flag was not planted on the moon. Chances are, you doubt the conclusion of this argument, and if so you can probably spot the weak premise. Why think that a flag could only wave that way if there were a wind? We can sensibly reject this argument at least until we are given some good reason to think that that premise is true.

A second argument: someone points out that a certain scientist doubts that global warming is caused by human beings, and concludes on that basis that global warming is a purely natural phenomenon. In this case, given the complexity and controversy surrounding the issue, we might wonder whether the testimony of just *one* scientist provides a whole lot of support for that conclusion.

In short, when evaluating particular arguments we can ask whether the premises are true, and whether the premises actually support the conclusion. Most arguments are more complex than the examples just given, but the fundamental strategies for questioning them are the same.

Philosophy of religion is filled with arguments, a number of which will be presented and discussed in the following chapters. Readers are encouraged to evaluate these arguments with care, and of course to apply this practice to everyday life.

Additional sources

In choosing terms, thinkers, and texts to highlight, I surveyed some of the good philosophy of religion anthologies currently on the market, to ensure that main topics covered there are also covered here. Three anthologies of note are:

Clark, Kelly James, ed. *Readings in Philosophy of Religion* 2nd ed. (Peterborough, Canada: Broadview, 2008).

Peterson, Michael L. et al., eds. *Philosophy of Religion: Selected Readings* 4th ed. (London: Oxford, 2009).

Pojman, Louis and Michael Rea, eds. *Philosophy of Religion: An Anthology* 5th ed. (Belmont, CA: Wadsworth, 2008).

In addition, the following text provides the historical background and development of many of the ideas and arguments that we shall discuss in what follows.

Zagzebski, Linda *Philosophy of Religion: An Historical Introduction* (New York: Blackwell, 2007).

Key Terms in Philosophy of Religion

Agnosticism

Agnosticism is a term that can be applied generally, and is simply a position that is midway between believing that something is true and believing that it's false. This may make agnosticism sound like a bad thing, so that an agnostic is wishy-washy, a fence-sitter; but that need not be so. We'd all agree that sometimes agnosticism is the appropriate position, as when the considerations that favor believing a proposition are exactly counterbalanced by considerations that favor believing that it's false. Likewise, if there is no evidence available either for the proposition or its negation, embracing agnosticism with respect to it seems like the sensible thing to do. Indeed, **evidentialism**, which claims that you must only believe what you have sufficient evidence for, may imply that agnosticism is often the rationally required stance for you to take.

A person can be agnostic about pretty much anything, but when we talk about agnosticism in philosophy of religion we typically mean agnosticism with respect to belief in God. A **theist** believes that God exists, an **atheist** believes that God does not exist, and an agnostic withholds belief and doesn't take a side. (There can be grades of agnosticism, where a person doesn't commit to theism or atheism but nonetheless leans to one side, perhaps judging it to be more likely than the other. Thinkers who lean toward atheism in this way are sometimes called atheists, when they are perhaps more accurately described as agnostic.) There can be lots of reasons for adopting agnosticism with respect to belief in God. A religious seeker may find compelling the famous arguments for God's existence—the **teleological** and **moral arguments**, for example—but may also find the **problem of evil** to provide powerful evidence that God does not exist. Or she may think that with our limited perspectives we simply cannot have sufficient evidence for or against the existence of a supposedly infinite and transcendent being like God. If so, agnosticism may be the most appealing and appropriate stance for her to take.

Analogy

Analogies are often employed in philosophical arguments, and this is no less true in philosophy of religion. In an argument from analogy it is noted that one thing is significantly similar to another thing, and that similarity serves as the basis for the argument that since the one thing clearly has a certain feature, the other thing probably has it, too. We can see this in a basic version of the **teleological argument**: the universe is like a machine; machines are the products of **intelligent design**; therefore the universe probably is, too.

The notion of analogy is important in philosophy of religion in another way as well. Philosophers have often wondered how we can speak about God, a being who, according to **theism**, is the greatest possible being, far greater than anything we can comprehend. If God is like that, how can our concepts even apply to God? Consider dogs, creatures that are considerably less intelligent than we are and whose conceptual schemes (ways of understanding and categorizing things in the world) are much simpler than ours. Surely dogs can't even begin to grasp what we are really like, and their ways of thinking about our cognitive, moral, and spiritual lives are bound to be pathetically limited. Don't those same considerations apply to us as we attempt to think about God?

A number of answers have been proposed. One suggests that our concepts apply to God literally, so that when we say that God is good, we are correctly applying to God the same concept of goodness that we apply to ourselves. An answer on the other side states that our concepts don't apply to God at all, so that we cannot express any positive truths about what God is like. (Perhaps we can only say what God is *not* like; this is the position of **negative theology**.) Any concepts we can come up with simply do not extend to a being so far beyond us.

The theory of analogy takes a middle ground between these two extremes. According to it, our concepts do not apply to God exactly as they do to us, but they do apply analogically. It's helpful to use dogs as an example again, though in a slightly different way. When we refer to a dog as "good" or "intelligent" we do not mean the same thing that we mean when we refer in that way to another person. Doggy intelligence and human intelligence are not the same thing. But the concepts are analogous, and a highly intelligent dog stands out among dogs in somewhat the same way that a highly intelligent human stands out among human beings. According to the theory of analogy, the same can be said of how our concepts apply to God. When we say that God is good, "good" should be understood as analogous to, but not identical to, the concept we apply to ourselves (and to other things). Thus we can in fact give useful descriptions of God even though our grasp of them, and our understanding of God, is bound to be limited.

Thomas Aquinas (1225–74) was a prime defender of the theory of analogy, and his defense can be found in ***Summa Theologica***, 1.13.5.

Apologetics

Apologetics is simply reasoned defense of a particular set of beliefs. Apologetics can be positive or negative: positive apologetics involves giving arguments in favor of one's particular set of beliefs, while negative apologetics attempts to refute arguments against them.

Contemporary readers may think that "apologetics" sounds, well, apologetic; but that's not how the term is used. It's helpful in this connection to think of **Plato's** (427–347 B.C.E.) great dialogue, *Apology*, where the apology in question is Socrates's defense of himself at his trial in Athens; and in that trial Socrates was certainly not apologizing for his behavior! Instead, he was giving an unflinching *defense* of it—an apology, used in the same sense as with the term "apologetics."

In philosophy of religion, many arguments for God's existence are referred to as part of theistic apologetics. Further, in Christian circles many apologists write in defense of specific Christian beliefs—in the resurrection of Jesus, for example. Key contemporary Christian apologists who specialize in both positive and negative apologetics and are prominent in philosophy of religion include **Richard Swinburne** (b. 1934) and **William Lane Craig** (b. 1949).

Atheism

Atheism is the belief that the God of **theism** does not exist. Atheists differ from **agnostics**, who believe neither that God exists nor that God doesn't. Atheists take the stronger stand and affirm that God does not exist.

Atheists give many arguments for their position. Historically the most signifi-cant has been the **problem of evil**. The existence of evil is powerful evidence that an omnipotent, omniscient, perfectly good being does not exist, so the argument goes. Other lines of reasoning in favor of atheism include the sug-gestion that the success of science, and perhaps particularly of the **theory of evolution**, indicate that God's activity is not necessary to explain anything in the natural world, and so we have no need to suppose that God exists. (Indeed, many atheists argue that the existence of God is ruled out by that theory.) Atheists have also sought to establish that the classic arguments for God's existence don't work; and some, particularly Antony Flew (b. 1923), have argued that we should start from a *presumption of atheism*, only accept-ing theism if its truth can be proven.

A number of objections have been posed to atheism, and perhaps the most important concern expressed about it is that atheism has unpleasant implica-tions for morality. Without God, critics fear, morality has no foundation: we have essentially no reason to care about what's right and wrong, and there may not *be* any right or wrong anyway. This fear was embraced by **Friedrich Nietzsche** (1844–1900), a German philosopher and atheist who explored the consequences of the "death of God." On his view, we need to understand that Christian morality (he called it *slave* morality), which glorifies weakness, meekness, and putting others before oneself, is dependent on belief in God and is therefore illegitimate and should be rejected. Other atheists part ways with Nietzsche on this point, however, and argue that we can make perfect sense of morality in a world without God, perhaps because human survival depends on our treating others with respect.

Atheism is as popular now as it has ever been, and there is no lack of book-length defenses of it. For a debate about God's existence between an atheist and a theist, see J. J. C. Smart and John J. Haldane, *Atheism and Theism* 2nd ed. (Malden, MA: Blackwell, 2003). For an attempt to counter the moral objection to atheism, see Kai Nielsen, *Ethics Without God* (Amherst, NY: Prometheus, 1990).

Calvinism

Calvinism is a branch of Protestant Christianity named after John Calvin (1509–64), from whose teachings the movement finds inspiration. When we talk about Calvinism in philosophy of religion, we are usually referring to a particular position on the nature of **divine providence** and human **free will**. This position will be our focus here, though we'll conclude with a note about Calvinist elements in another area of philosophy of religion as well.

Calvinism takes a very strong view of God's providence, and a correspondingly weak view of the role humans play in how things turn out. In essence, God has total control over everything that happens and has comprehensive knowledge of everything that is, was, and will be. (Thus Calvinism differs from both **Molinism**, which ascribes to God the same comprehensive knowledge but grants humans a greater role in determining what happens, and **open theism**, which denies that God has comprehensive foreknowledge.) This emphasis on divine sovereignty raises some obvious concerns about human freedom and moral responsibility.

One concern is this: if God controls everything that happens and, as a result, has comprehensive foreknowledge, then we cannot do anything other than what we actually do. We are simply playing the roles that are set for us; we are characters in a book that God has already written. If so, then how can we choose freely or be morally responsible for our choices? God does hold us responsible, at least for our sinful behavior, but how can that be just or fair if God also determines what choices we make?

The Calvinist response to this concern is to embrace **compatibilism**, the view which says that **determinism** and free will are compatible. In other words, Calvinists claim, your actions can be entirely determined by God and yet free if, for example, your actions are also caused by your own wants and desires. On this view, if you are sinning because you want to, then the fact that your actions are determined (so that you couldn't do or desire anything differently) doesn't matter. You are sinning freely, and hence you are responsible for what you do.

Still, if God determines everything that happens, then isn't *God* responsible for whatever happens, including your sinful actions and the suffering that results from them? This is a serious question for Calvinists because like all Christians they don't want to be committed to the view that God is to be blamed for evil. It is also a profoundly difficult question, and Calvinists have provided different answers to it. One answer suggests that God actively causes *almost* everything that happens, but when it comes to our sinful actions God does not cause them but instead merely *permits* us to do what our corrupt natures incline us to. Thus God does not cause us to sin and isn't blameworthy when we do.

This answer no doubt raises additional questions. But rather than explore them here, we should look briefly at two features of the typical Calvinist mindset that leads them into this conundrum and also allows them to remain at peace with it. The first is a strong commitment to the Bible as authoritative. On their reading, commitment to human responsibility and to a strong view of divine providence is simply non-negotiable, since both are taught in scripture (especially in the New Testament book of Romans). The second important feature of the Calvinist mindset is a willingness to accept the mystery inherent in some of the views they endorse. This willingness isn't groundless; instead it follows from recognizing the vast chasm between God's understanding and ours. Hence in cases where our sentiments, moral or otherwise, may chafe at what (on the Calvinist view) scripture teaches, we need to recognize that we are not in a position to question God or doubt what God has revealed to us. Ultimately we may have difficulty comprehending how such strong divine control over events meshes with human freedom and responsibility, but nonetheless they must mesh because the Bible teaches that they do. We must accept the mystery, and not allow the inability of reason to grasp it (and perhaps even the opposition of reason to it) to shake us from our faith.

Finally, while much discussion of Calvinism in contemporary philosophy of religion revolves around the issues of divine providence and human free will, Calvin's thought has had profound impact in other areas as well. The most important area is the theory of **Reformed epistemology** and its rejection of **evidentialism**, the requirement that belief in God be based on evidence. Readers are invited to turn to the Reformed epistemology entry to see something of Calvin's contributions there.

For a defense of Calvinism and discussion of objections to it, see Paul Helm's contributions to *Divine Foreknowledge: Four Views*, eds. James Beilby and Paul Eddy (Downers Grove, IL: InterVarsity Press, 2001).

Classical theism, see **theism**.

Compatibilism

Compatibilism is the thesis that **free will** and **determinism** are compatible. In other words, compatibilism claims that a person can have free will and can act freely even if all her actions are ultimately determined or caused by something outside of her control. That "something" is usually thought to be laws of nature—the laws of physics—or, as is widely discussed in philosophy of religion, God.

You may wonder why anyone would hold this view. After all, if the laws of physics, or God, determine everything that you do, then you cannot do anything other than what you do; and if so, how can your actions be free? If determinism is true then in every circumstance only one choice is available to you, and by choosing you simply find out which one that is. That doesn't sound like freedom! Yet a number of philosophers have accepted compatibilism, now and in centuries past. We should briefly consider two reasons that compatibilism might be attractive to them; then we'll turn to what freedom looks like from a compatibilist perspective.

One attractive feature of compatibilism is that it seems to provide the best of both worlds. The notion that the laws of physics causally determine everything that happens in the physical world is fairly plausible (at least with respect to larger objects like basketballs, if not to micro-particles like quarks). Besides, many religious believers, particularly proponents of **Calvinism**, endorse a strong view of **divine providence** which claims that everything that happens is essentially (perhaps with some qualifications) caused by God. So the thesis of determinism is quite popular. At the same time, almost everyone thinks that we have free will and that we are morally responsible for at least some of what we do. Compatibilism claims to give us a way to preserve both of these intuitions, a bit like having our cake and eating it, too.

A second reason that compatibilism is appealing is that serious questions have been raised about the main alternative to it. Proponents of **libertarian freedom** contend that compatibilism is false and hence that free action must be non-determined; but arguments have been put forward for the conclusion that non-determined free action is impossible. (For a brief summary of such arguments, see the libertarian freedom entry.) If that is correct, compatibilists say, not only is freedom compatible with determinism, it *requires* determinism. If we want free will, compatibilism is the only way to go.

What then does freedom look like on a compatibilist view? The simplest way to spell it out is that for compatibilists, you are acting freely if you are performing an action because you want to and not because you are being compelled to by some outside force. Thus, for example, if you go to class because you want to, you go there freely, "of your own free will"; while if you go only because your roommate forces you to at gun point, then you do not go freely. This account, compatibilists claim, accords with our ordinary way of speaking about free will: if you are acting on your own desires, most of the time we'd say that your actions are free.

The key point to understand here, the point that makes this account of freedom compatibilist, is that you can have this kind of free will even if everything you do is causally determined. It could be that all of the activity in your brain and all of your subsequent actions are under the sway of the laws of physics in the very same way that the motion of a basketball is, but that nonetheless sometimes you perform actions because you want to. Sometimes, in other words, your own wants and desires cause your actions. A person who knows absolutely everything there is to know about the laws of physics and the past state of the physical world could figure out exactly what menu item you will choose at Dairy Queen on some particular occasion, but this does not preclude your choosing a chocolate milkshake *because you want one*; and if you do so, then your choice is free. It doesn't matter that there is nothing else consistent with the laws of physics (or the decrees of God) that you could do, or that in an important sense you are "railroaded" into the choice that you make; it doesn't matter that your having the desires that you do is also causally determined. Your own desires cause your actions, and hence, says the compatibilist, those actions are free.

Compatibilism remains a highly contentious position, with its many critics contending that the freedom it offers isn't genuine freedom and isn't sufficient for moral responsibility. For a classic and accessible defense of compatibilism, see A. J. Ayer, "Freedom and Necessity," in *Free Will*, Derk Pereboom, ed. (Indianapolis: Hacket, 1997), 110–18. For an important critique, see Peter van Inwagen, "The Incompatibility of Free Will and Determinism," found in the same volume, 184–98.

Cosmological argument

The cosmological argument is one of the great arguments for God's existence—or, better, it's a great *kind* of argument, since there are many versions of the cosmological argument out there. In general, cosmological arguments consider the question, "Why does the world exist, anyway?" and arrive at the conclusion that God must be responsible for it and hence must exist, too. Here we'll look at two classic formulations of the cosmological argument and some objections to them.

Some of the most famous and straightforward versions of the argument are found in the "Five Ways" of **Thomas Aquinas** (1225–74), a much-anthologized excerpt from the *Summa Contra Gentiles*. The first argument we'll consider, his "second way," goes something like this.

1. Every event must be caused by another event.
2. The chain of causes cannot go back to infinity.
3. Therefore, there must be a First Cause, namely God.

Premise (1) is simply a statement of common sense, a version of what's called the *principle of sufficient reason*. No event just *happens*, this principle says; every event has a cause. This belief underlies our way of interpreting what goes on in our world. When a plane crashes, for example, everyone assumes that something *caused* the crash, and enormous resources are poured into determining the cause in order to prevent a similar accident in the future. So the first premise seems to be on solid footing.

Premise (2) claims that the chain of causes—where A was caused by B, which was caused by C, which was caused by D, and so on—cannot go back forever.

Well, why not? What's wrong with an infinite regress of causes? Aquinas says rather little about this in his short presentation of the second way, except to assert that if there weren't a first cause, there wouldn't be any other causes either. We may need more convincing on this point. Maybe it *is* a little strange to imagine a chain of causes not having a starting point, but the impossibility may not be so obvious that we can confidently hang an argument for God's existence on it.

We should note in passing that Aquinas actually meant something more complicated by the second premise than the simple reading we have been giving it, and that much more has been said in defense of that premise, too. (In particular, the **kalam cosmological argument** is dedicated to establishing that time must have a beginning, and argues in more detail—and in a way, interestingly enough, that Aquinas rejected—that an infinite regress of events is impossible.) But rather than exploring that complicated terrain, let us turn to a second version of the cosmological argument, one that does not depend on the assumption that there cannot be an infinite regress of events.

Our second argument comes courtesy of the German philosopher **Gottfried Leibniz** (1646–1716), and it builds from the version we just considered. Leibniz's point is that even if the chain of causes *does* go back forever, the existence of the world as a whole still requires an explanation. The world didn't *have* to exist; but then why does it? Leibniz argues that only God can serve as a sufficient reason for the existence of the world.

Before we proceed to spell out the argument, we need to draw an important distinction: the distinction between *contingent* and *necessary* things or beings (we'll use "things" and "beings" interchangeably). A contingent thing is a thing that exists but could have failed to exist. A necessary being, on the other hand, is a being that *must* exist; if there is such a being, it would be impossible for it *not* to exist. (A parallel distinction is made between contingent and necessary *truths*. Contingent truths are truths that could have been false, while necessary truths are truths that couldn't be. Most truths about events in the world are contingent since such events didn't *have* to happen, while most truths in mathematics, like that 2 + 2 = 4, are necessary truths.) With this distinction in mind, we should understand "the world" to be the collection of *all* contingent things; God, if God exists, is a necessary being.

The argument goes like this.

1. Every positive fact must have an explanation.
2. The existence of the world (the collection of all contingent things) is a positive fact.
3. Therefore, the existence of the world must have an explanation.

Let's pause to clarify. Note that premise (1) in Leibniz's argument is just another version of the principle of sufficient reason, but a stronger one than the one utilized in Aquinas's argument. Aquinas's argument depended only on the principle that every event must have a cause. With Leibniz we are stating that all *positive facts* have explanations. Anything that's true, anything that exists, there must be an explanation for why it's true or why it exists. Of course, we may not always know what the explanation is; but for every fact we always assume that there is one. The existence of the world is a positive fact, and so this version of the principle of sufficient reason implies that it requires an explanation.

The rest of the argument proceeds as follows:

4. The world (the collection of all contingent things) is a contingent being.
5. Only a necessary being could serve as a sufficient explanation for the existence of the world.
6. Therefore, a necessary being, namely God, exists.

Premise (4) claims that the world, the collection of all contingent things, could itself have failed to exist; here we can understand that to mean that there could have been no contingent things at all. Why then does the world exist? We have said in premise (3) that there has to be some answer to this question, some explanation for the existence of the world. What could it be? It's clear that the world's existence cannot be explained by a contingent being. After all, any particular contingent being is itself a member of the collection, and surely no one member of this collection can serve to explain the existence of the whole thing. Neither can the world explain its own existence, since no contingent thing can do that. (You can see this by reflecting on your own existence: you could have failed to exist, and something must explain how it is that you do exist—but that something can't be *you*.) So something outside the world, something non-contingent, must explain the existence of the world. The only option, as (5) says, is that a necessary being is responsible for it. Hence the conclusion: a necessary being, God, must exist.

The upshot of the Leibniz's cosmological argument, then, is that if any contingent things exist, then a necessary being must exist to serve as the ultimate explanation for the existence of the contingent things. This argument has been the subject of many objections, and here we'll consider three of them.

The first objection is often directed at any version of the cosmological argument. It comes in the form of an indignant question: But what about God? Don't we need an explanation for God, too? The answer: Yes we do, but fortunately one is immediately available. God is a necessary being, remember, and so the answer for why God exists is that God *has* to. (A similar explanation holds for necessary truths. Why does 2 + 2 = 4? Well, it *has* to; 2 + 2 simply cannot equal anything else.) God exists by God's very nature. No similar explanation applies to the existence of contingent beings, which is one key difference between necessary and contingent beings.

A second and more significant objection follows, however: are necessary beings even possible? Someone who doubts that there could be a being that simply *must* exist, whose non-existence is impossible, may find the cosmological argument dubious and may look for weaknesses in its premises. (It's interesting that this question, whether a necessary being like God is even possible, is one that also arises in connection with the **ontological argument**, and indeed may bring that argument down.)

A final objection to Leibniz's argument raises a question about premise (1) which, as we have seen, states a version of the principle of sufficient reason: all positive facts must have an explanation. Is that principle true? Can't there be *brute facts*, facts that simply are true and there is literally no explanation for them? (Perhaps the speed of light has no explanation in just this sense. Light travels at 186, 000 miles per second. Things could have been different—the fact that it travels at that rate is a contingent fact—but things simply *aren't* different and, on this suggestion, that is all that can be said about it.) If that is so, can't the existence of the world, contingent though it may be, simply be a brute fact? In other words, this objection claims, the principle of sufficient reason is not obviously true, and if it isn't true, then it is perfectly possible that there is simply no explanation for the existence of the world. The world just exists, and that is all there is to say about it.

Debate about the cosmological argument does not end here. For a Leibniz-style version of the argument, see Richard Taylor, *Metaphysics* 4th ed. (Englewood Cliffs, NJ: Prentice Hall, 1992) chapter 11. For a critique of the argument, see J. L. Mackie, *The Miracle of Theism* (London: Oxford, 1982), chapter 5.

creationism

Creationism is a controversial theory about the origins of the universe that has contributed quite a bit of heat to the debate over the relation between faith and reason, between **religion and science**. The term is used in several senses, but it is most commonly understood as the theory that God created all natural things in more or less their current form, at some time less than 10,000 years ago. This theory is rooted in a literal reading of the early chapters of the book of Genesis from the Christian (and Jewish) Bible, according to which God created the world in six days and rested on the seventh.

Creationism is not always distinguished from **intelligent design** (ID) theory, but it should be. Proponents of ID appeal to a variety of scientific evidence to try to show that the universe is the product of design, but the ID movement remains officially neutral on the nature of the designer and does not commit itself to defending a particular view of how the designer made the universe, especially not a view that runs as contrary to scientific orthodoxy as creationism does.

As a theory, creationism raises a variety of philosophical issues. The main ones have to do with the bearing that scientific research should have on religious belief. Should a person who believes that the Bible is inerrant (error-free) and teaches creationism be rattled by the pronouncements of contemporary scientists about the age of the earth? In a case like this, where faith beliefs clash with science, which one should give way for the religious believer? There are a number of options available. Some creationists have concluded that scientists are deeply misguided, because the earth looks much older than it actually is, or because of some anti-religious prejudices they have brought to their work, or because science simply cannot be trusted in this area despite its obvious success in others. Other creationists have attempted to show that science, done properly, actually *supports* their theory. But finally, many believers have concluded that their faith does not in fact commit them to the literal reading of Genesis that creationists espouse, and that it is open to them to learn from contemporary science about how God created the world. They take inspiration from the story of Galileo (1564–1642), who went against the Catholic Church by endorsing the view that the earth revolved around the sun, rather than the other way around. Galileo was forced to recant his view by church leaders who thought that the geocentric (earth-centered) theory was taught in scripture and essential to the Christian faith. Today, of course, Christians hold that there is no clash between faith and science on that point. Many Christians who do not accept creationism believe that the same reasoning applies here: Christian faith does not require belief in a young earth, and so there is no conflict here between faith and science.

Numerous books and websites are dedicated to this topic. An important book about the creationist movement is *The Creationists: The Evolution of Scientific Creationism* by Ronald L. Numbers (New York: Knopf, 1992).

Determinism

Determinism is the thesis that everything that happens and will happen is determined or set by what went before it. Events are thought to be determined by (1) the laws of nature or (2) God. Let's call the first *physical* determinism and the second *theological* determinism.

A helpful way to think of physical determinism is as follows: If physical determinism is true, then the complete physical state of the world at exactly midnight (Eastern Standard Time) 10,000 years ago today, together with the laws of nature, entails that there is only *one way* that things could go from there. To put it another way, the past together with the laws of nature determine one unique future. The history of the natural world is on an absolutely fixed track. For things to go any differently would require a violation of the laws of nature which, according to the thesis of physical determinism, does not and cannot happen.

Theological determinism, on the other hand, claims that all events are determined by God. On this view, God decrees that everything will go thus-and-so and ensures that everything goes that way, so that ultimately God is the cause of everything that happens and everything that happens is part of God's plan. We might think of God here as the all-powerful movie director who writes the script and causes everything to go in accord with it.

We should note, as an aside, that there is some debate over what would be sufficient for theological determinism to be true. Some people claim that God's merely *knowing* what will happen *determines* that it will, while others believe that God must not only know but must also *cause* those events to occur in order for their occurrence to be determined. This debate is relevant to the differences between **Molinism** and **open theism** on the nature of **divine providence** and **omniscience**.

A well-known question that arises with determinism is whether it is compatible with human **free will**. One view, appropriately called **compatibilism**, claims that you can be free even if determinism (physical or theological) is true, and a prominent theological tradition, **Calvinism**, embraces both (theological) determinism and compatibilism. (The thesis that both determinism and compatibilism are true is called *soft determinism*.) Other viewpoints, including Molinism and open theism, deny that determinism is true and also deny its compatibility with free will (they endorse the notion of **libertarian freedom**), while *hard determinism* accepts the truth of determinism but rejects its compatibility with free will, and as a result claims that free will is an illusion.

Divine command theory

Divine command theory (DCT) is a theory that provides an account of God's relation to morality, to what is morally right and wrong. We all know that some actions are right, which means we ought to (or may) perform them, and that other actions are wrong, which means we ought not to perform them; but thinking about this often raises the question, Why? Why ought I to tell the truth to my parents, and why may I not steal money from cash registers when opportunities to do so present themselves? The ultimate answer to these questions, according to DCT, is that God says so. On this theory, in other words, God gives us an answer similar to the one that many of us remember our parents giving when we asked too many questions about some course of action: "Because I said so!" Just as the buck stopped with our parents, on DCT the "moral buck" stops with God.

We can understand this theory a little better by considering it in connection with the **Euthyphro problem**. The Euthyphro problem raises the famous and important question, Is an action right because God commands it, or does God command it because it is right? DCT answers this question by taking the first option and saying that an action is right because God commands it. To put the matter very loosely, when God thinks about which actions to command and which to forbid, God does *not* say, "Hmmm. I see that truth-telling is right, so I'll command people to do that; lying is wrong, so I'll forbid it." Instead, on DCT, truth-telling isn't right *until* God commands it, and lying isn't wrong *until* God forbids it. God's commands *make* actions right or wrong. Thus God's choices of what to command and forbid are fundamental to ethics.

For **theists**, the DCT has much to be said for it. Intuitively, DCT gives God a significant role in morality, a role befitting the greatest possible being. If morality were outside of God's control, so that God had no say in what was right or wrong, that would seem to diminish God by putting God on a level with the rest of us who are subject to the demands of morality whether we want to be or not. Of course, God remains above us in both conveying to us the moral code and enforcing moral behavior; but still, those sympathetic to DCT argue, God's status requires more than that. God must not merely be the messenger and enforcer of the moral code, but also its author.

So, some of the reasons in support of DCT stem from reflection on the theistic understanding of God, and the worry that alternatives to DCT (that is, theories that say that God commands actions *because* they are right) have the unacceptable effect of compromising God's sovereignty. But some philosophers have also argued that DCT makes best sense of morality itself, and hence that certain features of the moral demand provide evidence for DCT. One such philosopher, **Robert Merrihew Adams** (b. 1937) claims that morality is both objective and non-natural. Moral truths like "slavery is wrong" do not depend fundamentally on how we think or feel about the world; instead, they are objectively true—they would be true even if none of us believed them. In addition, these moral facts are non-natural in the sense that study of the natural world will not reveal them to us. You can do scientific research as long as you want, but you will never discover what is right and wrong. Adams argues that these features of morality are best captured by DCT. God's commands, after all, do not depend on what we think or say, and hence they are objective. Moreover, they are not a part of the natural world, in so far as they are issued by a being who transcends it. Hence, Adams argues, reflection on the nature of morality yields good evidence for DCT. (Adams also turns this argument into a **moral argument** for God's existence, since if some actions are right and their being right depends on God's commanding them, that means that God must exist.)

Unfortunately, there are also some pretty serious objections to DCT. Here we'll focus on the most fundamental one, called the "arbitrariness" objection. We have seen that on DCT an action like telling the truth is morally right *because* God commands it, and likewise for any other right action. But what if God instead commanded *lying*? We think that God commands us to treat others with kindness and respect, and that doing so is morally right; but what if God commanded us instead to be nasty and rude at every opportunity? Even more disturbing, what if God commanded that we regularly torture defenseless persons just for the fun of it? DCT implies that all of those actions would then be morally right. But those actions, especially the last, simply *cannot* be morally right, and any theory that implies that they can be right must be mistaken.

The force of this objection can be seen further when we consider a knee-jerk response to the questions we just asked. We might think: of *course* God wouldn't command lying, nastiness, or such morally heinous behavior as torturing innocents for fun. God would never do something like that! But wait. Why not? What would stop God from doing this? It can't be the fact that such actions are *wrong*, since God's commands actually *make* them wrong. They aren't wrong until God forbids them. But why then did God forbid those actions? And here we see why this is called the arbitrariness objection: it seems like God had *no reason at all* to command particular actions or forbid them. Right and wrong are thus entirely arbitrary, rooted in the baseless whims of God. God could just as well have done things in reverse, commanding what God has forbidden, and forbidding what God has commanded.

Really, then, we have come upon two connected objections to divine command theory: it makes morality arbitrary, and it has the implication that such heinous actions as torturing innocents for fun could have been morally right. These are very serious problems with DCT, and most supporters of the theory have taken pains to respond to them. Here we need not detail the responses, except to say that they typically add to DCT the claim that there is *something* guiding God's decisions when it comes to commanding and forbidding. That way God's commands, and what is right and wrong, aren't entirely arbitrary, and moreover there is something that ensures that God does not command morally heinous actions. One example of a DCT that responds to the arbitrariness problem this way says that right and wrong are determined by the commands of a *loving* God, and such a God's commands would of course be guided by concern for the creatures to whom the commands were directed, a concern that would preclude commanding them to do terrible things to each other. To put the point differently, these types of DCT root right and wrong in God's commands, but then suggest that those commands are guided by God's good and loving *nature*. And this, they suggest, allows them to avoid the significant objections directed at less subtle and nuanced divine command theories.

For Robert Adams' explanation and defense of divine command theory, see "A Modified Divine Command Theory of Ethical Wrongness," in *The Virtue of Faith and Other Essays in Philosophical Theology* (New York: Oxford University Press, 1987), 97–122. For a recent variation on divine command theory, one which roots right and wrong in God's motivations rather than God's commands, see Linda Zagzebski, "The Virtues of God and the Foundations of Ethics," *Faith and Philosophy* 15 (1998), 538–53.

Divine hiddenness

Divine hiddenness is the notion that God is hidden, that the evidence for God's existence is not sufficiently compelling, and, perhaps more significantly, that many people who seek after God, who want there to be a God and want to believe, return from the search empty and disheartened. Divine hiddenness has recently been appealed to in powerful arguments for **atheism**. If God exists, then, being perfectly good, God must want to comfort and convince those who honestly seek after God. The fact that seekers come up empty indicates that God is not "hiding" after all; it indicates instead that God does not exist. In an interesting way, then, divine hiddenness arguments turn the apparent lack of evidence for God's existence into evidence against God's existence. Some philosophers, defending theism, have argued in response to this that perhaps the seekers are not appropriately prepared for the sort of relationship with God that God desires for people, and hence that God remains hidden from them until the time is right. Others suggest that with God being so far beyond us, we may simply be unable to comprehend God's reasons for hiding, just as we may not be able to understand God's reasons for allowing evil. For further development of the hiddenness argument and a response to it, see the exchange between J. L. Schellenberg and Paul Moser in *Contemporary Debates in Philosophy of Religion*, Michael Peterson and Raymond VanArragon, eds. (New York: Blackwell, 2003), 30–58.

Divine providence

This term refers to the way that God affects or controls what goes on in the world. In other words, it refers to the degree of sovereignty that God exercises in creation. There are different degrees of providential control that theists tend to ascribe to God. **Calvinism** takes a strong view of divine providence and holds that God controls everything that happens, essentially by causing it, except perhaps in the case of sinful human behavior. **Open theism** takes a weaker view and states that God allows human beings considerable autonomy to make their own choices and shape their own destinies, and that as a result God's intentions don't always come to fruition. A third view, **Molinism**, takes a middle position, suggesting that God grants humans some autonomy, but that God also knows what choices humans will freely make and controls events in light of that knowledge to ensure that human choices and events work together to fulfill God's purposes.

Dualism

As you may have suspected, this term refers to a view about "two" things. A number of dualisms are the subject of discussion in philosophy, but for our part we can just mention one very briefly and then spend most of our time on the most prominent theory that goes by the name.

The kind of dualism that we can cover briefly is sometimes called *cosmic dualism*, and claims that there exist two equal and opposed gods or forces that are together responsible for the way that the world is. One of these gods is good, one is evil, and neither is powerful enough to eliminate the other. A famous version of this theory is known as Manichaeism. It was endorsed for a time by **St**. **Augustine** (354–430); a discussion of it can be found in his book **Confessions**. For him, an important selling point for the theory was that it helped to explain the existence of evil: there is evil because the good god is limited in power and hence unable to stop the evil one from causing it. It is important to note that this sort of dualism is *not* endorsed by any of the major theistic religions—Christianity, Islam, or Judaism—and that Augustine ended up rejecting it partly because he concluded that ordinary **theism**, which claims the existence of a single all-powerful and perfectly good God, could explain the existence of evil at least as well. (Or, we should say, the "existence" of evil. Augustine believed that evil was not really an existing thing but was instead the mere absence of good. See the **theodicies** entry for more on his attempt to solve the **problem of evil**.)

On then to the more commonly referenced version of dualism, called *substance dualism*. This theory makes a claim about what human beings really *are*, when you get right down to it. Are you just a physical body, or maybe just a brain? (The theory known as **materialism** gives an affirmative answer to that question.) Or instead are you really a non-physical being that happens to be housed in a physical body? Substance dualism says that you are. In what follows we'll explore substance dualism a bit and consider some arguments for and against it.

According to substance dualism, there exist two kinds of stuff, physical and non-physical. Your body, like the rest of the natural world, is composed of physical stuff, but you are a non-physical thing. In other words, you and your body are different kinds of things. You are an immaterial mind or soul (we'll use these terms interchangeably)—or better, a *person*—that is housed in a physical body. You are in it, and you seem to be dependent on it in a variety of ways, but you are not identical with it. So says the substance dualist.

The appeal of substance dualism for religious believers—especially those who believe in human **immortality**—is clear. It seems that if you just are a physical body, then when it gets destroyed, so do you. Most of our bodies ultimately end up deteriorating by the end of our lives and decomposing and returning to the earth afterwards. How can we survive that? Indeed, how can God bring us back to life if the particles that make up our bodies get scattered to the four winds after we die? Substance dualism provides an easy answer. We aren't identical to those bodies, so they can be destroyed while we carry on without them. When our bodies die, we can be taken from them into a joyous afterlife.

So that is a significant reason that Christians in particular have historically been strongly partial to substance dualism. (Christians aren't the only ones who have defended it: immortality and substance dualism were also defended by a famous non-Christian, **Plato** [427–347 B.C.E.], in his dialogue **Phaedo**.) But other arguments for substance dualism have been given as well, arguments that don't depend on particular religious commitments. Perhaps the most common arguments have tried to establish that you (and your mind) have properties or characteristics that physical things could not have. If so, then they cannot be the same thing. (A general principle about identity says that if X is identical to Y, then X and Y must have all the same properties.

If Paul is six feet tall and the thief is only five feet, then they have different properties, which means Paul is not the thief.) The great philosopher **Rene Descartes** (1596–1650) presented an argument of this sort when he claimed to recognize by reflection that *he* (a mind) didn't take up space, didn't have any shape, and couldn't be divided into parts. Since physical things do take up space, do have shape, and are divisible—and thus have different properties from him—Descartes contended that he could not be a physical thing. Additional arguments have appealed to apparent "out of body" experiences, and even to the mere possibility of such experiences, to show that substance dualism must be true.

But there are also significant arguments against substance dualism. On the immortality front, religious believers inclined toward materialism have begun to make the case that we can live on (or be resurrected) after death even if we are purely physical beings. In other words, they have tried to explain how you can survive the destruction of your body even if you are it. Here we cannot consider these attempts in any detail (though more discussion of them can be found under the materialism heading). Suffice it to say the success of these accounts would undermine a significant motivation for accepting substance dualism.

Other objections to dualism try to show that the theory should be rejected on its own terms. One well-known objection is this. Substance dualism, as we have seen, holds that you are a non-physical mind housed in a physical body. But how exactly are you related or connected to your body, and particularly to your brain? Most substance dualists have said that you *causally interact* with it. So, for example, when your stomach is empty, physical activity in your brain causes you (the non-physical mind) to feel hunger, after which you ponder your options and decide to get some potato chips; this mental activity then causes more physical activity in your brain which leads to your body lurching out of the easy chair and heading to the pantry. So we have two-way causal interaction: your physical body causes events in your non-physical mind, and vice versa. This interaction between mind and body is extremely tight and indeed absolutely remarkable when you think about it. But how is such inter-action even *possible*, on substance dualism? How can something non-physical have any causal effects at all on something physical? (Ghost movies, which deal in non-physical beings, often have this problem to contend with. Many just ignore it, but the appropriately named *Ghost* tackles it head on by having the deceased character, played by Patrick Swayze, learn from another ghost on the subway that he can causally affect the physical world if he just concentrates really hard. Interestingly enough, walking on the ground doesn't seem to require such concentration.) And why is it that the causal link between mind and body is so tight and pervasive that we actually lose our ability to reason well when we're sleep deprived, and lose consciousness when we're hit hard on the head? If you thought that people were merely non-physical souls housed in physical bodies, you'd probably expect the connection between mind and body to be looser than that. You'd also expect that brain research might indicate that something non-physical was interacting with the brain, perhaps by detecting *gaps* in the causal activity in the brain where the non-physical mind (whose activity would be beyond the scope of the research) was doing its thing. But no such gaps have been detected, and it appears that there is no scientific evidence that substance dualism is true. All of this together, critics contend, makes a pretty good case that substance dualism is false, and that materialism is true; and if so then it is more important than ever that religious believers should work to explain how immortality is compatible with materialism.

That, in short, is how the debate over substance dualism has gone. Given continuing progress in scientific understanding of the brain, this debate will no doubt remain fascinating for years to come. For a debate between a dualist and a materialist, see the Dean Zimmerman–Lynne Rudder Baker exchange in *Contemporary Debates in Philosophy of Religion*, Michael Peterson and Raymond VanArragon, eds. (New York: Blackwell, 2003), 315–43. (Note that Zimmerman defends what's called *emergent* substance dualism, which suggests that the soul is naturally produced by the developing brain, rather than being miraculously placed in or fused with the brain by God.) For a book-length defense of substance dualism, see **Richard Swinburne**, *The Evolution of the Soul* (New York: Oxford, 1986).

Epistemology

Epistemology is the branch of philosophy that explores the nature of knowledge and the requirements for rational or justified belief. The concerns of epistemologists regularly spill over into philosophy of religion, since religion involves holding beliefs—often beliefs that cannot be verified or checked in the way that scientific or mathematical claims might be—and so questions easily arise about whether those beliefs can amount to knowledge or whether holding them can be rational or justified. Thus many philosophers working in philosophy of religion have migrated to epistemology, and have taken general theories about justified belief from there and tried to apply them to religious belief.

Many entries in this book have a tie-in to epistemology, but two opposed theories about the requirements for justified religious belief, **evidentialism** and **Reformed epistemology**, provide a good place to start. For a fine general introduction to the subject, see Richard Feldman, *Epistemology* (Upper Saddle River, NJ: Prentice Hall, 2003).

Euthyphro problem

The Euthyphro problem is a dilemma that goes back to **Plato's** (427–347 B.C.E.) dialogue *Euthyphro*. In this dialogue, Socrates (469–399 B.C.E.) talks with a religious man named, you guessed it, Euthyphro, who is on his way to court in Athens to prosecute his own father for murder. He expresses a great deal of confidence that he is doing the right thing, which leads Socrates to ask him what right action is, anyway. (In the dialogue Socrates and Euthyphro actually speak in terms of "pious" or "holy" action, but since the contemporary discussion of the Euthyphro problem is usually phrased in terms of moral rightness and wrongness, we shall phrase it that way here. We shall also omit some of the details of their discussion in order to zoom in on the problem.) Euthyphro's response, roughly, is that what is right is what God commands. What follows is the question that captures the Euthyphro problem: Is an action right because God commands it, or does God command it because it is right?

Why does this question pose a *problem*? Well, in short, it does so because it traps us in a *dilemma*: there are only two ways to answer the question, and both ways seem bad. If you give the first answer and say that an act is right because God commands it (the answer given by **divine command theory**), then you are left with the *arbitrariness* problem, where right and wrong are generated only by the groundless whims of God. On the other hand, if you give the second answer and say that God commands an act because it is right, then it seems that you have made morality separate from God, so that God is irrelevant to it and even subject to it in a way that threatens God's sovereignty. An action is right for some reason having nothing to do with God's choices, on the second answer. The rules are written, and God just has to issue commands in accord with them.

The Euthyphro problem raises profound questions for theists about the relation of God to morality. Does God write the moral rules? If so, what, if anything, guides the writing? And if not, does God have any significant role to play with regard to morality? For a Christian perspective on some of these issues, see John Hare, *Why Bother Being Good? The Place of God in the Moral Life* (Downers Grove, IL: IVP, 2002).

Evidential problem of evil

The evidential problem of evil is perhaps better called the evidential argument from evil. It is a version of the **problem of evil** according to which the evil that we see provides good evidence that God does not exist. (This is a weaker claim than that proposed by the **logical problem of evil**, which argues that because God and evil cannot possibly co-exist, the mere fact that evil exists entails that God doesn't.) But it's not the mere existence of evil that causes the problem, it's the character of evil that does. The suffering we witness seems so vast, so unfair, so pointless—even more so when we factor in animal pain which, according to the **theory of evolution**, has been going on long before human beings were able to cause it, prevent it, or learn anything from it. The evidential problem of evil argues that these features of evil provide very good evidence that God does not exist.

The evidential problem comes in many forms, but one of the best-known versions comes courtesy of American philosopher William Rowe (b. 1931). His argument goes something like this. Imagine some case of suffering that seems utterly pointless. Consider, for example, a fawn, badly burned in a naturally caused forest fire, who suffers alone for days before dying. Can you think of a good reason that God could have for allowing such suffering? It's difficult to come up with one, a difficulty Rowe uses as evidence that there is no such reason. And even if there should happen to be a good reason for God to allow this particular fawn's suffering, Rowe continues, there are so many other seemingly pointless or gratuitous evils that do occur and have occurred; and it would be astonishing if there were good reasons for every one of *those*. So it's sensible to think that some evil is in fact gratuitous. But, and here's the second claim, if God exists, God wouldn't allow gratuitous evil. In other words, God would only allow evils such that God's allowing them is necessary for the production of some greater good or the prevention of some evil equally bad or worse. (The following evils might be seen as non-gratuitous: the suffering that results from a punch to the nose, if the only way God could prevent it is by violating the free will of the puncher; and the suffering that results from a person's illness, if allowing it is the only way for God to promote moral virtue in the lives of the sick person and her family and friends. In both of these cases we would think that God is justified in allowing the suffering, because allowing it serves a point.) God wouldn't stand idly by, allowing suffering for nothing. After all, God is supposed to be perfectly good, and it would be a sign of moral weakness if one were to allow preventable evil for no good reason. Since there is gratuitous evil, and there wouldn't be if God existed, we must conclude that God does not exist.

It might be helpful to spell this argument out.

1. There is gratuitous evil.
2. If God existed, there wouldn't be gratuitous evil.
3. Therefore, God does not exist.

It's important to stress that the reason this is called an *evidential* argument from evil is that premise (1) is based on the evidence of some of the evil we witness, and in particular on the fact that we cannot think of any good reason God could have for allowing it. That is, some of the evils we contemplate *seem* gratuitous, and that is good evidence that they really *are* gratuitous.

Or is it? At this point some defenders of **theism** have stepped in and argued that the fact that these evils, like the suffering of the fawn, seem pointless or gratuitous gives us no reason to think that they are in fact gratuitous.

No doubt if God exists, they say, God would have reasons for acting (and permitting) as God does, and chances are that many of these reasons would be entirely beyond us. We are, after all, considerably less intelligent and well-informed than an omniscient being like God would be! But then the fact that we cannot see why God, if God exists, would allow these seemingly gratuitous evils doesn't give us any good reason to think the evils really *are* gratuitous. Chances are that if God existed we still wouldn't understand, and thus the evils would still seem pointless to us.

An analogy might help us to understand this response to the evidential problem of evil a little better. Think for a moment about very young children and their parents. Parents are typically much more intellectually advanced and better informed than young children are, and sometimes parents have to do things that cause their children grief, for reasons that the parents understand but the children cannot. Consider, for example, the vaccination shots to which infants are regularly subjected; and let's imagine that a particular infant (with narrowly focused but unusual intellectual capacities) reasoned about the experience as follows: "My parents are allowing me to experience this terrible pain, and I cannot see why they would do so. The fact that I cannot see why they are allowing this gives me good reason for thinking that there is no reason and that my suffering is gratuitous. But if my parents loved me, they wouldn't let me endure gratuitous suffering. Therefore, my parents don't love me." The proper response to such a child (who is, of course, incapable of understanding the parents' actual reasons) would be to say that the evidence adduced for the premise that the suffering is gratuitous is not good evidence for it, since the suffering would seem that way to the child even if the parents actually had good reason to allow it. And that is the same response that our defender of theism has given in response to the evidential problem of evil. As infants are to their parents, so we are to God (except that the intelligence gap in the second case is far greater). Just as the infant should not infer much from his inability to see the reasons his parents might have for allowing his suffering, so we cannot justifiably infer much from our inability to see the reasons God might have for allowing particular evils. The child's inability certainly doesn't give him good reason to think that his parents don't love him, and likewise our inability doesn't give us good reason to think that God does not exist.

This response has prompted a great deal of discussion, and readers are encouraged to read further and attempt to determine its success. It's worth noting, too, that this response to the evidential problem of evil is a *defensive* one: it simply attempts to thwart the evidential argument from evil by showing that we don't have good reason to think that premise (1) is true. But theists might instead attempt to give a more aggressive and ambitious response: they might try to supply plausible reasons for God to allow those evils. That is what **theodicies** try to do: they try to explain why God allows evil. A complete theodicy, presumably, would explain why God allows helpless fawns to suffer, and would also explain why God permits all of the truly **horrendous evils** that we witness in this world. Theists differ in their optimism about our ability to understand God's purposes, and some believe that the defensive response to the evidential problem of evil is probably the best one we can give.

For more, see William Rowe's essay, "The Problem of Evil and Some Varieties of Atheism," *American Philosophical Quarterly* 16 (1979), 33–41, reprinted in many anthologies. It contains the version of the evidential problem discussed above. The response is based on Stephen Wykstra's, "The Humean Obstacle to Evidential Arguments from Suffering," *International Journal for Philosophy of Religion* 16 (1984), 73–93. Additional essays on the topic, many quite accessible, can be found in *The Evidential Argument from Evil*, Daniel Howard-Snyder, ed. (Bloomington: Indiana University Press, 1996).

Evidentialism

Evidentialism is actually a position in **epistemology**, the field of philosophy that studies the nature of knowledge and rational belief. Evidentialism is the view that in order to be justified in believing something—in order to believe it rationally—you must believe it on the basis of evidence. (Evidence here typically means an *argument*, though what can constitute evidence is itself a matter of debate among evidentialists.) The key is that we must have reasons for what we believe, reasons for thinking that those beliefs are *true*; and it is irrational and maybe even wrong to hold beliefs without them.

One strong and influential version of evidentialism was put forward by **W. K. Clifford** (1845–79) who claimed that we have a moral duty to believe on evidence. His mantra, proclaimed in his essay, "The Ethics of Belief," was this: "It is always wrong, everywhere, and for anyone, to believe anything on insufficient evidence!" When proclaiming this he did not state explicitly that he had *religious* beliefs in mind, but most people have thought that he did, since such beliefs are often held without evidence of the sort Clifford appeared to be looking for.

Thus evidentialism, though it presents us with a general claim about justification for *all* beliefs, very often is applied specifically to religious beliefs, and particularly to belief in God. That's why it is such a central topic in philosophy of religion. It poses a challenge to theistic belief, a challenge that can be put in terms of an argument as follows:

1. If there is insufficient evidence for God's existence, then it is wrong or irrational to believe that God exists.
2. There is insufficient evidence for God's existence.
3. Therefore, it is wrong or irrational to believe that God exists.

If this argument is sound, then you shouldn't believe in God. But of course many people *do* believe that God exists, and wouldn't be happy with the conclusion that it is wrong or irrational for them to do so. They will want to reject the argument, and the sensible way to do so would be to question one of the two premises. (Another way to reject an argument is to show that the premises don't support the conclusion; but with this argument they clearly do.) To question premise (1) is to question evidentialism itself, and many philosophers have done just that. Some have proposed **pragmatic arguments for belief in God**, which provide reasons to believe in God in the absence of good evidence, reasons which usually involve practical benefits that can be gained by believing. Others have defended **Reformed epistemology**, which claims that we can justifiably *start* with belief in God, and don't have to provide evidence or arguments for it.

Some philosophers and theologians have also attacked premise (2) of the evidentialist challenge by putting forward arguments for God's existence. In other words, they argue that there *is* sufficient evidence for that God exists, and hence that we can be perfectly justified in believing in God. This attempt to come up with sufficient evidence for God's existence is known as the project of **natural theology**.

Evidentialism thus touches on many debates in philosophy of religion, some of which are discussed in more detail elsewhere in this book. It also touches on a central issue of the discipline, the relation between faith and reason. Evidentialism claims that faith beliefs, like all beliefs, are not properly held unless they are supported by evidence, and in doing so, it takes a stand with **rationalism** in giving reason priority and authority over faith.

Evolution, see **theory of evolution.**

Evolutionary argument against naturalism

The evolutionary argument against naturalism is a provocative argument recently put forward and defended by **Alvin Plantinga** (b. 1932). **Naturalism**, the target of the argument, is the claim that the natural world is all that there is, and that there exist no gods or supernatural beings of any kind. The main point of the argument is to establish that any naturalist who reflects on the origin of our cognitive faculties—those faculties that produce in us all of our beliefs, like the belief that grass is green, that 2+2=4, and that France is a country—should come to doubt everything she believes, including naturalism itself.

The argument goes like this. If naturalism is true, then human beings almost certainly came to exist by way of the mechanisms described in the **theory of evolution**—by random genetic mutation acted on by natural selection. This evolutionary process produced all of our traits and capacities, including our cognitive faculties; and it did so without being guided by anyone, since on naturalism there is no one to guide it. Now, an important thing to recognize about the process of evolution is that it is fundamentally concerned with how we *behave* rather than with what we believe. If a tiger is after you, it's what you *do* rather than what you believe that's going to enable you to survive (or not). You could believe all sorts of crazy things, but if it results in appropriate tiger-avoidance behavior (running away, for example), then you pass that particular evolutionary test. This means that our cognitive faculties were *not* selected by the evolutionary process primarily because they produced true beliefs in us, beliefs which accurately describe the way the world is; instead, our cognitive faculties were selected primarily because they helped us to survive. But this raises a question: if that is how our cognitive faculties came to be, and again if there were no supernatural beings guiding the process, what is the likelihood that our cognitive faculties actually *do* get us true beliefs? How probable is it that they are reliable?

In fact, Plantinga argues, that probability is quite low (or else it's inscrutable—we just can't tell what it is). His argument for this is a tad complex, but here's the idea. We should think first about the link between our beliefs and our behavior, and note that there are two ways that this link can go: either (1) our beliefs actually impact our behavior (as we usually think they do—we usually think that your belief that your car is in the parking lot helps cause your body to walk over there), or (2) they don't. Now, Plantinga argues, it is difficult to see on naturalism how beliefs *could* impact behavior (that is a philosophical puzzle of the first order), and there is actually a reasonable chance if naturalism is true that (2) is correct and our beliefs have nothing to do with how our bodies behave. And if our beliefs don't impact behavior, and evolution cares only about how we behave, then evolution doesn't care one bit what we believe. We could believe any old thing and it wouldn't have any effect whatsoever on whether we survive or not. But then our evolutionary origins wouldn't make it likely at all that our cognitive faculties get us true beliefs—indeed, it would be quite likely that they don't! So, if (2) is correct, then the probability that our cognitive faculties get us reliably in touch with the truth would be very low.

Admittedly, it would be quite surprising if our beliefs really don't have any impact on our behavior. So let's suppose that they do—let's suppose that (1) is true—while noting that naturalism has a difficult time accounting for how this could be. It seems that if our beliefs affect our behavior, and we have to behave appropriately in order to survive, then it's somewhat more likely that our beliefs would be true given that we have survived. If we had mostly false beliefs, and those beliefs caused our behavior, our behavior would have led to our extinction, wouldn't it? Well, maybe not. As Plantinga points out, all sorts of false beliefs can contribute to behavior that promotes survival. (One of his examples: you believe that the presence of a tiger signals the start of a race, and so as soon as you see one you run as fast as possible in the other direction. Your belief is false, but it helps you survive.) So, on option (1), Plantinga argues, the probability that our faculties are reliable is only moderately high. It's certainly not a sure thing.

At this point, supposing for now that given naturalism it is just as likely that our beliefs impact our behavior as that they don't (so that (1) and (2) are equally likely to be true), we should average the probabilities that our faculties are reliable on each option in order to determine the overall probability, on naturalism, that our faculties are reliable. The average of moderately high from option (1), and very low from option (2), is still quite low; and this is exactly Plantinga's conclusion. A naturalist should thus conclude that it is quite unlikely that her cognitive faculties are reliable, and correspondingly quite likely that they are not.

Now, Plantinga says, the naturalist has a problem. For it seems that anyone who has this sort of reason to think that her cognitive faculties are unlikely to deliver her true beliefs should refrain from believing anything that her cognitive faculties tell her—which is *every belief she has*, including naturalism and evolution. It would be irrational for her to continue to accept the deliverances of faculties she believes are unreliable! It would be just like you believing the testimony of a friend you think lies most of the time. So, Plantinga concludes, reflective naturalists who accept the evolutionary explanation of human origins (no other explanation seems available to them) should be skeptical about every belief that they entertain.

This argument has been quite controversial, for it seems to have the implication that we need to believe that our cognitive faculties were designed by some benevolent supernatural being (like God), in order to rationally trust those faculties. (This line of reasoning has been put forward before, particularly by **Rene Descartes** (1596–1650) who concluded that he could trust his cognitive faculties because God created him and wouldn't let him go wrong if he used them properly.) Some philosophers have responded to Plantinga by arguing that the process of evolution could likely by itself, without divine oversight, furnish us with reliable cognitive faculties. For critical discussion of this argument, including objections and Plantinga's replies, see *Naturalism Defeated? Essays on Plantinga's Evolutionary Argument Against Naturalism*, ed. James Bielby (Ithaca, NY: Cornell, 2002).

Exclusivism

Reflection on **religious diversity**—the fact that there are many different major religions in the world, with millions of adherents some of whom display a great deal of spiritual and moral sensitivity—often leads to the question whether different and apparently opposing religious traditions can be inspired by the same divine reality, and whether each can provide a genuine path to salvation. Exclusivism, as we'll use the term here, answers both questions in the negative. (Two views that differ from exclusivism include **inclusivism**, which claims one religion is true but that members of other religious groups can nonetheless be saved, and **pluralism**, which sees different religions as tapping the same divine source and leading to the same end.) According to the exclusivist, only one religion is true and only its adherents can attain salvation. In what follows we'll discuss a Christian brand of exclusivism; note that other religious groups can and do endorse exclusivism as well.

According to Christian exclusivism, Christianity is the one true religion, the one religion that correctly describes the divine reality and our relation to it. All the other religions are mistaken, perhaps on many issues, but certainly on any points where they conflict with Christian belief. Moreover, only people who explicitly believe the central Christian truths at the time of their deaths can achieve salvation. (Some exceptions are often added, typically for children of believers who die young and for biblical persons who served God faithfully before Jesus arrived.) All others will spend the afterlife in eternal **hell**.

Christian exclusivism, implying as it does that unbelievers are eternally damned, provides a strong motivation for its adherents to do mission work—to get out into the world, spread the religious message, and turn unbelievers into believers. And of course Christians have historically placed a strong emphasis on evangelism. That emphasis can sound arrogant and intolerant given today's sensibilities, but it's worth noting that with exclusivism in the background, winning converts is a profoundly moral thing to do, since it helps gain salvation for those who would otherwise be damned.

Exclusivism has been popular among Christians, but it certainly has its critics. When considering it, one wonders why God, who by all theistic accounts is perfectly good and by Christian lights is fundamentally characterized by love for the people God created, would restrict salvation to so few people and allow so many people to be damned. This is even more troubling when we think about how many people never get a legitimate chance to take on the faith that is necessary to salvation, since so many people never hear the Christian message or hear it only in a distorted form. Further, many other religious systems seem to be of real benefit to their adherents, many of whom seem to be genuinely in touch with the divine. Are we to think that that benefit is ultimately weightless, and that all of these people, despite their apparently admirable moral and spiritual qualities, are bound for hell because they don't have the right beliefs? Many critics of exclusivism find the problems that these questions raise to be insurmountable, and in general exclusivism is probably not as dominant a position among Christians as it once was.

Yet it retains its supporters. Christian exclusivists, even while recognizing the difficulties, typically believe that the Bible teaches exclusivism, and hence that it must be true even if they are not able to understand how or why. This response in the face of apparent philosophical difficulties again calls to mind the issue of the relation between faith and reason. When should philosophical reflection prompt us to give up some belief that up to that point we believed to be a dictate of divine revelation? There is much disagreement among religious believers over how to answer this question.

Additional resources: helpful debate about Christian exclusivism can be found in *Four Views on Salvation in a Pluralistic World*, Dennis L. Okholm and Timothy R. Phillips, eds. (Grand Rapids, MI: Zondervan, 1996). Note that there the position is called "particularism." A defense of a different kind of exclusivism—the view simply that one's own religious beliefs are true—is found in **Alvin Plantinga's** "A Defense of Religious Exclusivism," from *The Rationality of Belief and the Plurality of Faith*, Thomas D. Senor, ed. (Ithaca: Cornell University Press, 1995) and reprinted in many philosophy of religion anthologies.

Existential problem of evil

The existential problem of evil is the problem that many people encounter when they witness or experience horrific suffering. A poignant example of this can be found in Fyodor Dostoevsky's *The Brothers Karamazov*, in a chapter called "Rebellion," where one brother, Ivan, describes to another some appalling cases of child abuse. Ivan's deeply personal reaction to the events he recounts is rebellion against the God who permitted them to happen. The story reveals something of the way that evil can turn people away from God; it can lead people to question God's existence or renounce previous religious commitments; it can have a powerful, faith-shattering effect on people who experience it. (Evil can also turn people *to* God: sometimes people who suffer horribly find their religious faith strengthened as a result. But this does not happen in every case.)

Notice that the problem here does not take the form of an explicit argument as the **logical** and **evidential problems of evil** do. The person suffering doesn't carefully draw conclusions from his experience. Instead, the response tends to be more passionate and immediate; and because of this some philosophers have wondered whether philosophy can be of any help with the existential problem of evil. **Alvin Plantinga** (b. 1932), for example, has suggested that this is a "pastoral" problem, and that people experiencing it— people who find themselves struggling with their religious faith as a result of suffering—need spiritual counseling rather than rigorous philosophizing. **Marilyn McCord Adams** (b. 1943), on the other hand, has argued that philosophy can be of assistance here, and much of her own work in philosophy of religion has involved spelling out ways that God might defeat **horrendous evils** by ensuring that the lives of those who experience them are on the whole worth living.

Powerful expressions of the impact of evil are found in great literature all over the world. Two books of note (excerpts of which often appear in philosophy of religion anthologies) are Albert Camus, *The Plague* (New York: Vintage, 1991 [1947]) and Elie Wiesel, *Night* (New York: Hill and Wang, 2006 [1958]).

Feminism and philosophy of religion

An important aim of feminism in general is to uncover biases and prejudices that contribute to unjust social arrangements and the oppression of women. Feminist thinkers have used this approach in thinking about religion—and rightly so, given the disheartening tendency of some religious groups both now and in the past to explicitly or tacitly assign to women second-class status. A common target for feminists in philosophy of religion has been the concept of God, particularly as it has been picked up in the Christian tradition. Christians often refer to God in masculine terms: they refer to God as "Father" and emphasize God's superiority and power. Doing so, some feminists argue, has promoted the patriarchal notion that males are more God-like and ought to be in charge. In *Sexism and God-Talk* (Boston: Beacon Press, 1983), Rosemary Radford Ruether (b. 1936) mentions that theologians have usually believed that our concepts do not apply to God literally anyway, and certainly not in the case of gender; and she argues that speaking inclusively and recognizing feminine characteristics of God will give us a fuller picture of God and will help us to work against patriarchy and sexism.

For more on feminism and philosophy of religion, see Ruether's book as well as Patricia Altenbernd Johnson, "Feminist Christian Philosophy," *Faith and Philosophy* 9 (1992), 320–34.

Fideism

Fideism is a theory about the relation between faith and reason, and it raises the former (*fides*, in Latin) above the latter. According to fideism, faith, whose source is divine revelation, is to be trusted over reason, which has limits and perhaps is even corrupted by sin. (**Rationalism**, on the other hand, trusts reason over faith.) There are different ways that fideists understand the nature of the relation between faith and reason, and accordingly different versions of fideism.

An extreme version, as we said in the first chapter, truly disparages reason. It claims that reason should not be applied to matters of faith at all, because to subject religious beliefs to philosophical scrutiny implies a lack of trust in the source of those beliefs, and reason cannot help us to understand the claims of faith anyway.

More moderate versions hold reason in somewhat higher regard, while maintaining the primacy of faith. They differ on such issues as whether reason conflicts with faith, and on the degree to which reason can comprehend or support faith claims. Danish philosopher **Soren Kierkegaard** (1813–42) believed that reason conflicted with faith in that by reason's lights such events as the incarnation (where God became human) could not happen; and he said that we must take a "leap of faith" to accept that it did. Other fideists hold that while reason does not directly conflict with faith, rational methods cannot (and need not) be used to show that faith beliefs are true. Reason can be used, however, to help us comprehend the claims of faith, if only in a tentative and limited way. On this view, reason is faith's servant. This position, captured by the slogan "faith seeking understanding," was famously endorsed by **Augustine** (354–430) and **Anselm** (1033–1109). We can see it at work in Anselm's ***Proslogium***, where he employs reason to understand God's existence and attributes, and also states that reason unguided by Christian faith will inevitably lead us astray.

For a good and accessible discussion of fideism, see C. Stephen Evans, *Faith Beyond Reason: A Kierkegaardian Account* (Grand Rapids, MI: Eerdmans, 1998).

Foreknowledge, see **omniscience.**

Free will

Free will involves our ability to make choices in such a way that we are the authors of them and are morally responsible for making them. Free will is the subject of enormous controversy in philosophy. One major debate is between those who think that free will is compatible with **determinism** (so that our actions can be causally determined yet still free) and those who think it is not. (**Compatibilists** believe that the two are compatible while advocates of **libertarian freedom** deny this.) This debate is relevant to philosophy of religion because of its connection to debates over the nature of **divine providence**, where theists disagree over how to square God's activity in the world (and God's **omniscience**) with human free will and responsibility. The notion of free will also plays an important role in discussions of the **problem of evil**, since many theists think that the existence of free will helps explain why there is evil and why God allows it. See the collection *Free Will*, Derk Pereboom, ed. (Indianapolis: Hackett, 1997) for classic and contemporary readings on the subject.

Free will defense

The free will defense is a response to a specific version of the **problem of evil**, known as the **logical problem of evil**. The characters in this story are **J. L. Mackie** (1917–81), who forcefully presented the logical problem, and **Alvin Plantinga** (b. 1932), who developed the free will defense to refute it.

Mackie's logical problem of evil is really just an argument for the conclusion that God does not exist. The argument claims that it is impossible for God and evil to co-exist, since if God existed God would eliminate all evil (being **omnipotent**, God would be able to; being **omniscient**, God would know how to; and being **perfectly good**, God would want to). Since evil clearly does exist, it must be that God does not.

The free will defense constitutes a response to this argument. Its aim is modest: to show that it is in fact possible for God and evil to co-exist. The easy way to do that is to describe a *possible situation* in which God and evil co-exist. If such a situation is in fact possible (if it could possibly occur), then it is possible for God and evil to co-exist; and if so, then the contention that such co-existence is *im*possible is mistaken and the logical problem of evil has been refuted.

We can understand Plantinga's free will defense by first clarifying two assumptions he makes. First, there all sorts of **possible worlds**—all sorts of ways that things could be. (In the actual world, Barack Obama is elected president in 2008, but things could have been different, meaning that, for example, in many possible worlds he loses that election and in many possible worlds he doesn't even run.) Some of these worlds may seem better than the actual world (it seems that things could be better than they are), while others seem considerably worse. If God exists, then God would only actualize a really fine world; it would be beneath God, inconsistent with God's goodness, to create a really despicable or even a mediocre world. The second assumption is that morally significant **libertarian freedom** is a valuable thing, so that all else being equal, a world containing creatures with the freedom to choose between right and wrong is better than a world containing only complex robots following a program.

Now in light of those assumptions, Mackie's argument is essentially this: if God exists, then God must create the *best* possible world, namely, *a world with freedom but no evil*. But how might God create a world like that? God couldn't just create free creatures and then always *compel* them to freely do what's right, because if God compels them, then their actions are not free. (If God gives creatures libertarian freedom, then what they do is in an important sense not up to God.) Maybe so, says Mackie. But surely there are possible worlds in which all creatures blessed with significant moral freedom *always* freely do what's right. They have the sorts of moral choices that we have, but when they face those situations they, unlike us, *always* freely make the right choice. In a world like that, creatures enjoy morally significant freedom, but there is no evil. (No moral evil, and presumably no natural evil either—no suffering caused by floods, earthquakes, or incurable diseases.) If God exists, God must create such a world; thus since such a world is not actual, it must be that God does not exist.

Enter Plantinga's free will defense. The intent of the defense is to show that it is possible that God in fact could *not* create a world with freedom but no evil. To set up this possibility, we should first understand the notion of *transworld depravity*. If a person, Hugh, suffers from transworld depravity, then for *any* world God could create, if God puts Hugh in it (and gives Hugh morally significant freedom) then Hugh will freely sin at least once, thereby introducing or contributing to the evil in that world. So, if God wants to create a world with freedom but no evil, God knows that Hugh is one person God can't put in it, because no matter what the world is like, Hugh would mess it up.

The thing to see is that it's possible for there to be people like Hugh who suffer from transworld depravity and, if they do, there is nothing God can do about that. What people will freely do in any particular set of circumstances is not up to God. As we have said, God can't compel Hugh to freely do what's right. God could, however, *refrain* from creating Hugh; and if God wants to create a world with freedom but no evil, God might very well do that.

Here's how the notion of transworld depravity fits into the free will defense. We have acknowledged that it is possible for someone like Hugh to suffer from transworld depravity. The next step is to see that it is also possible that *every single person that God could create* suffers from it. And note what would happen if this possibility were actual: then God would be *unable* to create a world in which there is freedom but no evil. There would be no one whom God could put in such a world. If every possible person suffered from transworld depravity, then prior to creating anything God would know that any person God puts in the world would mess it up just like Hugh would. Thus, since it is possible that every person God could create suffers from transworld depravity, it is possible that God couldn't create a world like the one Mackie insisted God would have to.

If so, must God refrain from creating altogether? The free will defense continues: surely not, since a world with freedom and *some* evil may be a sufficiently good one for God to create. And if so, then we have arrived at a possible situation in which God and evil co-exist. In it, all people God can create suffer from transworld depravity, yet God elects to create a world with free people knowing they'll do wrong and cause evil. Since this situation is possible, we have shown that it is in fact possible for God and evil to co-exist. We have refuted the logical problem of evil.

Two final points must be made about the free will defense. First, it is essential to understand that the free will defense is *not* a **theodicy**. It makes no attempt to explain God's *actual reasons* for allowing evil. Its goal, instead, is entirely defensive (hence its name): the logical problem of evil launches an attack on theistic belief, saying that it's impossible for God and evil to co-exist; and the free will defense thwarts that attack by showing that it's not impossible after all. It is no part of the free will defense to claim that all people God could create really *do* suffer from transworld depravity, and that's why God created a world with evil; the free will defense simply claims that that *could* happen, and if so, then that would give God a good reason to create a world with evil.

Second, the defense as stated depends on the theory of **divine providence** known as **Molinism**. (Perhaps it can be stated in a way that doesn't depend on Molinism.) According to Molinism, God knew prior to creating the world what free choices creatures would make in any situation that God might place them in. You can see the role that this theory plays in the free will defense: if God is to know that every creatable creature suffers from trans-world depravity, God has to know what free choices they would make before God decides whether to create them. Molinism is a fascinating theory in its own right, and readers are invited to turn to that entry for more information about it.

For development of the logical problem of evil and a full version of the free will defense, see Mackie's much anthologized "Evil and Omnipotence," *Mind* 64 (1955), 200–12, and Plantinga's *God, Freedom, and Evil* (Grand Rapids: Eerdmans, 1977).

God, see **theism**.

God and time

Practically all theists believe that God has always existed, that God thus has no beginning and no end, and further that God is a necessary being, a being that simply must exist in the very same way that 2 + 2 must equal 4. They disagree among themselves, however, on God's relation to time. Some believe that God is outside time, or, as it is said, "timeless", "atemporal," or "eternal"; on this view, God doesn't experience time passing the way we do, but instead somehow experiences all of it at once. Others believe that God is inside time and is merely "everlasting," without beginning of end. The former view was once standard among theists, particularly among medieval theologians, but today the latter view has become quite popular as well. In what follows we'll look at some of the debate surrounding both positions on God's relation to time.

To understand the appeal of a timeless God, we should see how it fits with the view of God as the epitome of perfection. Early Christian thinkers, like **Augustine** (354–430), took inspiration from Greek philosophy as they reasoned through what a perfect God must be like. The ancient Greeks, following **Plato's** (427–347 B.C.E.) statements in the dialogue *Timaeus*, believed that a perfect being must be both timeless and changeless (immutable). These features come as a package: if God exists from moment to moment in time, then God must change, at least in so far as God constantly changes beliefs about what time it is; and if God changes then at one moment God is one way and at the next moment another, which means that God must be in time. As the Greeks saw it, to change ill befits a perfect being, since change involves getting better or worse: if a being gets better, it wasn't perfect before, and if it gets worse, it isn't perfect now. Early Christians were influenced by these kinds of considerations and were led by them to postulate that God is changeless and outside time. Rather than being swept along by time like we are, God created time and transcends it.

Aside from fitting well with Greek notions of perfection, the idea of God outside time has been thought to help us make better sense of how divine foreknowledge and human freedom fit together. As Boethius (ca. 480–525) points out in **The Consolation of Philosophy**, if God sees all time at once, then God doesn't see your actions in advance, God sees them all *now*; and just as someone else's seeing you perform an action as you perform it doesn't threaten your freedom, God's seeing you perform that action from the vantage point of eternity doesn't threaten your freedom either.

Nonetheless, there are difficulties with the notion of God being outside time, and these have led many philosophers and theologians in recent years to postulate that God is in fact inside time. First, it is hard to see how it would work for God to create time from outside it. (Thinking about creation raises the question: what was God doing *before* creating time; and of course if God was doing anything before that, then God was already in time!) This is one of many straightforwardly philosophical concerns about the idea of God outside time. Second, there are questions about whether an eternal God can fit with the portrayal of God in the Bible. There God is described as acting in the world, responding to prayer, and changing over time—but how can these descriptions be correct if God is outside time? Third, there are concerns about the pastoral value of a timeless God. Of what use to us in the face of the world's suffering and evil is a God who remains unaffected, unchanged, viewing all of time at once and hence experiencing it in a way unimaginably different from the way that we do? Difficulties like these have led many Christian philosophers to reject the atemporal view of God as an illegitimate import from Greek philosophy into Christianity, and have prompted them to take some of the biblical language about God more literally than theologians of past centuries have done.

The debates over God's relation to time lead straight into fascinating questions about the nature of time itself. Is all of time real, or is only the present real? (If only the present is real, does that rule out the possibility of time travel? There would be nowhere—or no-*when*—to go!) Is the passage of time an illusion? Some of these issues are taken up, and variations on the two views just discussed are defended, in Gregory Gannsle, *God and Time: 4 Views* (Downers Grove, IL: InterVarsity Press, 2001).

Hell

In Christian thought, hell is the place where people who do not attain salvation spend eternity. (According to **universalism**, no one will end up spending eternity in hell and everyone will eventually attain salvation; but universalism has always been a minority view among Christians.) There are many philosophical concerns about hell, including questions about what it is like, who ends up there, and why God (being **perfectly good** and loving) allows such a place to exist. Here we shall briefly explore two kinds of answers to this question. Keep in mind that many variations on these views are possible.

The first view is a strong one. It sees hell as a place of punishment, where sinners (the ones who do not believe in Jesus Christ and hence whose sins are not paid for by his atoning sacrifice on the cross) suffer physical and emotional torment for all of eternity. God permits the existence of hell and the suffering of its inhabitants because that suffering is just, in so far as any sin at all is a grievance against an infinite God and hence is deserving of infinite punishment.

The second view is more moderate. Hell remains a place of punishment, but the punishment is largely self-imposed. By making self-centered, sinful choices, its inhabitants shape their characters in such a way that heaven ends up not appealing to them. God loves those in hell but also respects their freedom, and as a result lets them exile themselves to a hell which they actually prefer to heaven. They never achieve anything like genuine happiness and they do not flourish the way human beings are intended to; but to some degree they are blind to their plight and thus their suffering is not as intense as that described in the strong view.

There are numerous objections to both views. Critics of the strong view claim that its hell is unjust and barbaric. Critics of the moderate view argue that it doesn't fit with the portrayal of hell found in the Bible, and that no one could genuinely choose hell over heaven. For an evaluation of the strong view, see Kelly James Clark, "God is Great, God is Good: Medieval Conceptions of Divine Goodness and the Problem of Hell" in *Religious Studies* 37 (2001), 15–31. For a defense of the moderate view, see Jerry Walls, *Hell: The Logic of Damnation* (Notre Dame, IN: University of Notre Dame Press, 2001). See also

C. S. Lewis's *The Great Divorce* (San Francisco: HarperOne, 2009 [1945]) which tells a story that amounts to a description of the moderate view, where a bus from hell visits heaven and many of the passengers do not wish to stay there.

Horrendous evils

As you'd expect, this term refers to really bad evils. But it has also been given a technical sense in philosophy of religion by **Marilyn McCord Adams** (b. 1943). For her, horrendous evils are evils that give those who participate in them good reason to think that their lives on the whole cannot be worth living. The examples Adams cites are indeed horrendous: the rape of a woman and axing off of her arms, slow death by starvation, participation in the Nazi death camps. These are horrendous evils in that they call into question the overall good of the lives of the participants, both victims and perpetrators.

A key reason for highlighting horrendous evils is to make clear the seriousness of the **problem of evil**. How can the creator God truly love all people, while at the same time allowing evil to harm some individuals so badly that it would have been better for them had they not been born? Adams' contention is that any complete and successful theistic response to evil must focus not only on the global goods that God attains by allowing evil—that is, not just on the goods for the world as a whole (the preservation of human free will, for example)—but must also explain how God might defeat horrendous evils in the lives of the individuals who experience them, so that their lives are in fact worth living despite those experiences. This issue has been a regular theme in Adams' writings, but the most thorough discussion of it can be found in her book *Horrendous Evils and the Goodness of God* (Ithaca: Cornell University Press, 2000).

Immortality

Many religious groups believe in human immortality—they believe, that is, that we live on after our earthly deaths. Christianity, Islam, and Judaism hold that we enter an afterlife after death, perhaps heaven or **hell**, while Buddhism and Hinduism adopt a doctrine of reincarnation according to which after bodily death we are reborn as other creatures or persons, in other bodies. (This process will not go on forever, but the important point is that earthly death is not necessarily the end of us.)

An important philosophical problem that the notion of immortality raises is this one: how is it even possible for us to survive our deaths? To put the problem in theistic terms, how can God ensure that you—the very person who is reading this book—make it to heaven after your bodily existence ends on earth? The answer to this question, of course, is going to depend on what *you* really are. Two prominent theories have been proposed (though there are others). First, according to substance **dualism**, you are an immaterial soul housed in a material (physical) body. If so, when your body dies you can be whisked off to heaven and your soul placed in another body. Second, according to **materialism**, you actually are your body (or some part of it). This would seem to present serious obstacles to immortality, since if you are your body and your body dies, you die, too. Religious materialists argue, however, that these obstacles can be overcome, and they also claim that other philosophical and scientific considerations speak strongly in favor of their view.

Inclusivism

Inclusivism is a response to the question of **religious diversity**—the question of what to make of the many different religious traditions and their devoted followers—that takes a middle position between **exclusivism** and **pluralism**. The exclusivist says that only one religion is the true one and that only its adherents can attain salvation. The pluralist says that all major religions constitute appropriate responses to the same Ultimate Reality, and that they all lead to the same end. The inclusivist, on the other hand, claims that only one religion is the true one, but that members of other traditions might still achieve salvation even if their religious beliefs are mistaken.

To make the discussion concrete, here we'll speak specifically of Christian inclusivism. (Analogous positions could be drawn up from the perspectives of other religions.) Christianity teaches that God became human in the person of Jesus Christ, was executed by crucifixion but then arose from the dead, thereby conquering death and making possible our salvation. Many Christians are exclusivists and hold that this salvation is available only to believers; but Christian inclusivists reject this picture as being deeply unfair to those who never hear the gospel, and out of step with the biblical picture of a loving God who desires the salvation of everyone. Somehow, inclusivists insist, there must be a way for non-Christians to be saved.

What is the way? Inclusivists agree with exclusivists that the Christian story is true, of course; and so they affirm that the *fact* of the death and resurrection of Jesus is essential to our salvation. But they deny that explicit *belief* that these facts are true is likewise essential. A standard inclusivist suggestion is that there can be people who do not hear the Christian story but who respond as best they can to whatever awareness they do have of God and God's demands on them. In other words, a person raised on a remote island in the south Pacific might have some feeling that there is a divine power and a moral law that he ought to follow, and might respond appropriately to those feelings and seek to live in accord with them. On the inclusivist picture, God may be working through such a person. Indeed, the person could appropriately be referred to as an "anonymous Christian," and hence may be in a position to achieve salvation without actually hearing or believing the Christian claims about Jesus.

To sum up, inclusivists believe that their religious tradition is uniquely correct and at the same time that persons who are members of other religious groups may yet be saved. This puts them between exclusivists and pluralists; and attacks have come from both sides. Exclusivists argue that the inclusivist position can make no sense of the need to engage in evangelism. Pluralists argue that once we have granted that salvation can come to members of other religious groups, there is no good reason left to claim, as inclusivists do, that our own religion is uniquely true.

These issues are profound and are only becoming more relevant in today's world, as religious groups grow increasingly intermingled and the question of how they should think about their differences becomes more pressing. For a defense of inclusivism, see Karl Rahner, "Christianity and the Non-Christian Religions" in *Christianity and Other Religions*, John Hick and Brian Hebblethwaite, eds. (Oxford: Oneworld, 2001), 19–38. Inclusivism is depicted in fiction by **C. S. Lewis** in the book *The Last Battle*, the final installment of his Narnia series, where the world ends and a follower of Tash, the false god of the Calormines, finds himself in heaven with the lion (and Christ character), Aslan.

Intelligent design

Intelligent design is the name of a movement whose aim is to provide scientific evidence that the world is the product of design rather than chance. In essence, ID involves drawing out new versions of the **teleological argument** (also called the argument from design), and it opposes **naturalism** and the view that the **theory of evolution** can by itself provide a complete explanation of the history of life on earth.

One prominent ID argument is presented by Michael Behe (b. 1952) and makes use of the notion of *irreducible complexity*. Science, Behe tells us, reveals that some cellular structures are irreducibly complex, which means that all their parts are essential to them in such a way that if they were reduced by any single part they would be functionally useless. This poses a problem for the theory of evolution. That theory claims that life developed gradually by way of genetic mutation acted on by natural selection. Organisms are sometimes born with characteristics that their ancestors lacked, and, roughly speaking, new characteristics that promote survival are passed on to descendents, and those that do not are not. The problem is that it's difficult to understand how this process could produce irreducibly complex structures. Consider one such structure, the mammalian eye. The process of evolution doesn't produce complete eyes all at once; but anything less than a complete eye would fulfill no function that could promote the survival of creatures that have it. But then how could evolution produce the eye? Behe concludes that supernatural activity was probably involved in its production, and hence that the eye, together with all other irreducibly complex structures of living organisms, is probably the product of intelligent design.

Other ID arguments aim to show that the improbable events that have come to pass in the production and development of life on earth should be attributed to intelligent design rather than chance. An example of such an argument comes courtesy of William Dembski (b. 1960). If you flip a coin 100 times, he points out, whatever ordering of heads and tails turns up was in fact equally (and incredibly) improbable, whether they all land heads or whether forty-three of them do. Despite this, if they all land heads we assume something fishy is going on, and we don't attribute that ordering to chance. But why not? Dembski suggests that we quite properly infer design in the all-heads case because that ordering is *specified*—it conforms to an independently established pattern—while orderings we would ascribe to chance are not. Much of Dembski's work has been dedicated to spelling out the conditions under which design can be scientifically detected, and arguing that design can be detected in the natural world.

The ID movement has been a lightning rod for criticism. Against the arguments just presented, critics have claimed that scientists are beginning to understand how evolutionary processes might produce cellular structures which are supposedly irreducibly complex, and that Dembski's formula for design detection is seriously flawed. The movement gets criticism on political grounds as well. Some proponents have tried to get ID taught in public school science classes in the United States. Opponents argue that ID doesn't belong there because it is not science: it produces no explanations that might yield predictions and open doors to further experimentation and research. (Critics have also claimed that ID is simply **creationism** in disguise; but it's important to note that unlike creationism, ID makes no attempt to show that the earth is less than 10,000 years old, and also does not officially take a stand on the nature of the designer.)

Discussion of the ID movement abounds in books, journals, and on the internet. Behe's book *Darwin's Black Box* (New York: Free Press, 1996) has produced many responses, including Philip Kitcher's "Born-Again Creationism," in *Intelligent Design Creationism and Its Critics*, Robert T. Pennock, ed. (Cambridge, MA: MIT Press, 2001). Dembski has written many books, including *The Design Inference* (Cambridge: Cambridge University Press, 1998). For a critique of that book, see Robin Collins, "An Evaluation of William Dembski's *The Design Inference*," *Christian Scholar's Review* 30 (2001), 329–41.

Kalam cosmological argument

The kalam cosmological argument is a fascinating proof for God's existence that turns on the notion of infinity and attempts to show that the world must have had a beginning. It was developed in medieval times by Islamic philosophers and revived recently by **William Lane Craig** (b. 1949). In what follows we'll work through his version of the argument.

The main argument actually consists of two distinct parts, each of which is sufficient to establish the conclusion. The first part turns on the distinction between an *actual* infinite and a merely *potential* infinite. An actual infinite is a collection or set that contains infinitely many things, while a potential infinite is always increasing but never reaches infinity. So, to illustrate, we may think that the set of natural numbers contains infinitely many numbers—an actual infinite—but if you start at zero, count one number every second, and carry on counting without end, at any point you will only have a potential infinite, never an actual one.

Now suppose you hold that the universe was not created or started by anyone, and that, in some form or other, history goes back forever and ever, with no beginning. Perhaps you think that our universe began with the Big Bang and will eventually end with a "big crunch" (that is, it will eventually collapse back on itself), and that prior to our universe there was another universe that started and ended the same way, and before that another and another and another, going back forever. (This picture of the history of everything, known as the *oscillating universes model*, is almost certainly not accurate, but it was once quite commonly accepted and now gives us a helpful way of thinking about the matter.) If you think that, then it seems that you are committed to believing that *infinitely many events* have happened before now. That is, imagine that all the events that have existed before now compose a collection or a set: those events constitute an *actual infinite*. (Or think of the infinitely many years that have taken place before now, or, on the oscillating universes model just presented, the infinitely many universes that have existed prior to the one we're in.) And this is where the *kalam* cosmological argument gets going: how could there *be* an actually infinite collection of things?

After all, when you think about it, actual infinites are pretty crazy. We might see this by considering "Hilbert's Hotel," named for the German mathematician David Hilbert (1862–1943) who spent a lot of time thinking about these things. Suppose that a hotel contains infinitely many rooms—an actual infinite—and suppose all the rooms are full. Up to the hotel comes a car with one passenger. He enters the lobby and asks for a room. "We're completely full, but we still have room for you!" the attendant responds cheerfully. The attendant promptly goes to the first room and asks the guest to move to the next room; then everyone gets moved one room over, and the new guest sets up in the first room, stretches out, and goes to bed. Two strange features of this situation: no one loses a room, and after we have added a guest there are no more people in the hotel than there were before. (There are still infinitely many.) Crazy! In fact, we can change the situation to make even clearer the absurdity of an actual infinite. Suppose that a bus drives up loaded not with one but with infinitely many passengers. The driver asks the hotel attendant if his passengers can each get a room, and the attendant gives the same answer as before: "We're full, but we still have room for each of you!" Then the attendant makes rooms available for them, as follows: The guest in the first room is moved to the second; the one in the second is moved to the fourth; the one in the third is moved to the sixth; and so on so that the room number of each guest is now twice what it was before, and all the odd-numbered rooms are empty. Since there are infinitely many odd-numbered rooms, all of the passengers on the bus can now get some rest. And the same features remain: no one loses a room, and even though we have added infinitely many guests to the hotel, there are no more in it now than there were before.

You can see how reflections like these could make one reject the possibility of an actual infinite. (Perhaps we can make an exception for abstract objects like numbers. The natural numbers make up an actual infinite. But it's crazy to suppose that more concrete things like events or universes could compose an actual infinite.) Recall that if the world has no beginning, it follows that an actual infinite (of events, universes, or some such thing) must exist. If an actual infinite *can't* exist, then it seems that we must conclude that our world had a beginning. And that is precisely what the *kalam* cosmological argument intends to show.

Suppose, however, that you're not yet convinced. Maybe you think that even if they are crazy, actual infinites may still be possible, and so we haven't successfully established that the world must have a beginning. Fortunately, as we said, this argument has two parts. If you haven't accepted the argument of the first part, there's another one. The second part of the argument does not assume what the first part attempted to establish, namely, that actual infinites are impossible. It tries in a different way to show that the world must have a beginning.

Think about this. Imagine that the world in fact has no beginning, and thus that infinitely many events have occurred before now. Given this assumption, a question arises: how did we get to *now*, to the present? Well, the events that have made up the past constitute a collection that has been formed by successive addition: there was one year, then another, then another . . . and eventually we got to this one. But if there was no beginning and hence infinitely many years before now, that means that we must have crossed infinitely many years, one by one, to get to this point. And that's impossible! Getting to the present in a beginningless world would be like jumping out of a bottomless pit. Hence, if there were infinitely many years before now, we couldn't have gotten to the present. We are in the present, so there couldn't have been infinitely many years before now; instead, there must have been a beginning to time. And again, that's what the *kalam* cosmological argument is intended to show.

So, there must be a beginning because either (1) actual infinites are impossible which means a beginningless world is impossible or (2) a beginningless world would make it impossible to get to the present, which is something that we have obviously done. So says the argument. But of course the conclusion that the world has a beginning is a far cry from the conclusion that God exists. This argument must therefore be supplemented with more steps. Since the additional steps are not exactly part of the historical argument (though they are developed by Craig and others), here we'll just indicate briefly how they go.

The next step is to show that the beginning of the world must have a *cause*. This step appeals to the principle of sufficient reason which undergirds the ordinary **cosmological argument**, and the essential point of it is this: a world can't just pop into existence out of nothing; there must be some reason or explanation for its coming into existence; and the only suitable explanation is that something outside the world, and outside of time, caused it to exist.

But why think that the something that caused the world to exist is anything like the God of **theism**? Well, the world is itself a causal chain, a chain of events that has a starting point. What kinds of things do we know of that start causal chains like that? Why, people like us, of course. (An aside: the notion that people start causal chains in this fashion is often endorsed by proponents of **libertarian freedom**, particularly those who explain that freedom in terms of what's called *agent causation*.) But then the sensible thing to think is that the world was also caused by a person, though a supernatural one, one outside the world and outside of time; and of course that's God. So, working from our initial conclusion that the world has a beginning, we have inferred that God exists.

There is much more to say about this intriguing argument. Questions have been raised about each step. Readers are invited to study the argument and ponder the following questions. Do examples like Hilbert's Hotel give good reason to think that actual infinites are impossible? If the world has no beginning, does it follow that we have crossed infinitely many years to get to the present? Does the proposed alternative to a beginningless world, one where a timeless being started the world, face any similar problems? For a thorough defense, see William Lane Craig's *The Kalam Cosmological Argument* (Eugene, OR: Wipf and Stock, 2000); see also Paul Draper, "A Critique of the *Kalam* Cosmological Argument," in *Philosophy of Religion: An Anthology* 5th ed., Louis Pojman and Michael Rea, eds. (Belmont, CA: Wadsworth, 2008), 45–50.

Libertarian freedom

In the debate over the nature of human **free will**, there are two main combatants: defenders of **compatibilism** and defenders of libertarian freedom. Here we'll look at what libertarian freedom is, at one objection to it, and at how it figures in other debates in philosophy of religion.

Freedom, libertarians say, requires the ability to do otherwise. If your choice to pick up this book and read it was a free one, then at the moment you did so you were genuinely able to refrain and do something else instead (say, pick up a different book, or go watch television). And the important point for libertarians is this: freedom is incompatible with **determinism**, so that if your actions are caused by physical laws or by God, then you do not have the ability to do otherwise and you are not acting freely. (On this point, libertarians disagree with compatibilists.) Thus God cannot control what you do, cannot compel you to act in some particular way, without compromising your freedom. Libertarians insist that only non-determined actions can be genuinely free, and we can only be morally responsible for the consequences of that kind of action.

The libertarian contention that free action must be non-determined is the source of the principle objection to their theory. If an action is not causally determined—if the events that precede it do not guarantee that it will happen—then, so the objection goes, the action is simply random. In fact, it's not properly called an action at all; instead, it is something that just happens, a chance event. (Think of some neurons in your brain firing randomly, without being caused to do so, and causing your left arm to flail out. The movement of your arm is non-determined alright, but it is certainly not a free action.) The challenge for libertarians, in the face of this objection, has been to explain how an action can be non-determined but also non-random.

One popular libertarian response to this challenge has been to propose the notion of *agent causation*. Most people believe in *event* causation—they believe, in other words, that events cause other events. But some libertarians suggest that *agents* can also serve as causes, that agents can be the originators of causal chains in the world. Hence when you perform an action, on this picture, you are the agent-cause of it. Your action does have a cause and hence isn't random, but it was caused by *you*, and not simply by events in your brain, or, for that matter, by God. (In fact, some libertarians have suggested that our powers as agents are similar to God's: just as God initiates causal chains and performs actions that are not causally determined by any outside events or forces, so do we.)

The notion of libertarian freedom, while intuitively plausible, is clearly a vexed one. We should highlight two areas of philosophy of religion where it plays a central role. Libertarian freedom is front and center in theistic debates about the nature of **divine providence** and **omniscience**, and their impact on free will. In those debates **Calvinists** reject libertarian freedom while **Molinists** and **open theists** endorse it. It is also important to theistic responses to the **problem of evil**. Free will often plays an important role in **theodicies**, the idea being that God allows evil because God chose to create people with free will and hence cannot control what they do. But this idea only works if God gives people *libertarian* freedom, since God *is* able to control what people with compatibilist freedom do. (Remember: on the compatibilist picture, you can act freely even if God determines how you will act.) Thus a standard theistic response to the problem of evil seems to require that we postulate that we have libertarian freedom; the problem becomes even more complex without it.

For further reading about libertarian freedom and some of the puzzles that surround it, see Peter van Inwagen's chapter "The Powers of Rational Beings: Freedom of the Will" in his book *Metaphysics* 3rd ed. (Boulder, CO: Westview, 2008) 253–72.

Logical problem of evil

The logical problem of evil is a forceful argument for the conclusion that God does not exist. It claims that we can logically deduce that conclusion from the mere fact that there is evil. After all, the argument goes, if God exists, then God is **omnipotent**, **omniscient**, and **perfectly good**; and as such, God is able to eliminate evil, knows how to eliminate evil, and wants to eliminate evil. Hence, if God exists, there would be absolutely no evil—it would be contrary to God's nature to allow it. Yet clearly there *is* evil. It follows in a most straightforward fashion that God does not exist.

The logical problem of evil is not as widely discussed today as it once was; most philosophers now consider the **evidential problem of evil** (which contends more moderately that the amount and kinds of evil that we witness constitutes good evidence that God does not exist) to be much more promising. The reason that the wind has gone out of the sails of the logical problem is that the **free will defense** is widely understood to constitute a successful response to it. Details about the free will defense can be found elsewhere in this chapter; suffice it to say that it's rooted in the notion that God, though perfectly good, could conceivably want to allow creatures **libertarian freedom** even if doing so will bring evil into the world.

Materialism

The term "materialism" is used in many senses in philosophy. Sometimes it is used to denote the global claim that everything that exists is physical, composed of matter. This view is sometimes called *scientific materialism*, since it comes with the suggestion that science, which studies the physical world, is essentially studying all that there is and hence should be seen as our primary road to truth.

Here we'll consider a narrower use of the term. Materialism in the sense we'll explore makes a claim only about *us*, a claim about what human beings are. It claims that we are purely physical (material) creatures; we are not, as substance **dualism** asserts, non-physical souls attached to physical bodies. We *are* physical bodies, or perhaps some part of them. Materialism thus understood is opposed to substance dualism, but, unlike what we just called scientific materialism, it is compatible with **theism**. You can be a materialist in this sense and believe that an immaterial God exists; you just cannot at the same time believe that we are in some way immaterial ourselves. Materialism is probably the most popular view about the nature of human persons in the Western philosophical and scientific communities, and it is also becoming increasingly popular among religious philosophers.

There are a number of general philosophical concerns with materialism, as well as specific concerns generated from religious commitments. One general concern, from the field of philosophy known as philosophy of mind, is the problem of *intentionality*. According to materialism, our minds are purely physical, which means that our beliefs, fears, and desires are all physical things or physical events that occur in our brains. But it is difficult to understand how this could be. Beliefs, fears, and desires, after all, have intentionality, which is to say that they are *about* things and *refer* to things outside themselves. Perhaps you have the belief, for instance, that the University of Notre Dame has a decent football team—that belief is *about* Notre Dame and its football team. But how can a physical thing or a physical state be about or refer to anything? That is to say, how can it have intentionality? Consider the chair you're sitting in right now: that chair is not *about* anything. True: brains are more physically complex than chairs are; but how should that make any difference? It's not like you can take a physical thing, make it more and more complex, and suddenly it starts referring to the University of Notre Dame! Thus the idea of mental states like beliefs, fears, and desires being purely physical is a deeply puzzling one.

The primary religious concern with materialism is that it is often thought to rule out the possibility of **immortality**, life after death. If you just are this physical organism (your body), and the organism is blown up in an explosion and scattered to the four winds or, less dramatically, dies a normal death and decomposes in the ground, it is difficult to see how both it and you (since you are it) could ever be brought back to life. Since, as we have noted, many Christian philosophers have tended toward materialism is recent years, a good deal of scholarly energy has been dedicated to solving this problem. Here we'll briefly indicate a couple of (probably) unsuccessful solutions, which serve to clarify the main issue that an acceptable solution must address.

The situation, then: you are a physical organism, and you have just died. How is God going to raise you from death and bring you into the next life? A first possibility is that God might make a physical duplicate of you. At the moment of your death, your body (which is you) had a certain physical composition, and God, knowing it in every detail, could simply make a copy, plunk that up in heaven, and there you are! Sadly, this won't work: the obvious problem is that a copy of you isn't really *you*, so while the result may be some contented person wandering around heaven thinking he or she is you, that person would be mistaken and you would in fact no longer exist. (There are other problems, too: if it's a copy of your body as it was right at the moment of your death, wouldn't the duplicate immediately die like you did?) A second possibility, then, is that God might recover all of the actual particles that made up your body at the moment of death, haul them to heaven, and put you back together there. Pretty clearly God doesn't do this immediately, since bodies don't vanish right after they die; so if God takes this option, there must be a waiting period between death and "re-constitution." But there's a problem: what if the particles that made up your body before your death are in use by someone else when God goes to retrieve them? Particles get recycled, after all: our bodies decompose and become part of the soil, which becomes part of the plants that grow in it, which become part of the animals that eat them, which become part of us! What would God do if that were to happen? For reasons like this, it's unclear whether this second plan would be any more workable than the first one.

In short, the challenge for materialists who believe in life after death is to explain how a person in the afterlife can be connected to you in such a way as to *be* you, rather than some deluded copy of you. Again, much work has been done to explain how this might work. For a clear discussion of these issues and a rejection of the possibility of immortality, see John Perry, *Dialogue on Personal Identity and Immortality* (Indianapolis: Hackett, 1978). For a Christian defense of materialism, see Kevin Corcoran, *Rethinking Human Nature: A Christian Materialist Alternative to the Soul* (Grand Rapids, MI: Baker, 2006).

Metaphysics

Metaphysics is a central branch of philosophy that aims to discern the reality underneath all appearances. It's helpful to compare metaphysics with **epistemology**: epistemology studies the nature of our knowledge of reality, while metaphysics attempts to discern the nature of reality itself. The problems in metaphysics (as with most problems in philosophy) cannot be resolved purely through the acquisition of scientific knowledge, though such knowledge can provide direction. One can see this when considering the many questions in metaphysics that are also questions in philosophy of religion. For example, does God exist? Does substance **dualism** accurately capture the true nature of human persons, or does **materialism**? Is **determinism** true? Do we have **free will**? Scientific evidence can be adduced to support different positions but, most people suspect, it cannot settle these debates.

An introduction to metaphysics that includes excellent discussions of the above topics is Peter van Inwagen, *Metaphysics* 3rd ed. (Boulder, CO: Westview, 2008).

Methodological naturalism, see **naturalism**.

Middle knowledge, see **Molinism**.

Miracles

Miracles are usually thought of as violations of the laws of nature caused by divine intervention in the natural world. The following events are examples of miracles: the changing of water into wine; a person walking on water; and a person coming back from death to life. In each case, physical laws dictate that the events in question will not happen, so when they do happen, those laws are violated. Miracle stories are important to many religions, especially to Christianity which claims a miracle—the resurrection of Jesus—as the central event in human history.

The concept of a miracle raises many philosophical questions, but here we'll focus on a salient one: Can it be rational to believe that miracles actually happen? An initial reason for doubting that it can has to do with success of modern science. We have often seen, with the advance of scientific thinking, cases where phenomena that once puzzled people, phenomena that people explained by reference to the supernatural, are now understood and explained in purely natural terms. (For example, what was once called demon possession is now explained as mental illness.) Perhaps our scientific understanding of reality should make us shun appeals to divine intervention and rest assured that natural explanations are available even if we do not know yet what they are.

But what about those really spectacular events that clearly do not admit of natural explanations, like the miracles just mentioned? The great skeptic **David Hume** (1711–76) offered a powerful argument that we shouldn't believe that such events have ever happened. We should only believe what we have good evidence for, he contended; and we always have stronger evidence against any particular miracle story than we have in favor of it.

His argument goes like this. The fact that miraculous events run so counter to our ordinary experience (in our experience water doesn't instantly transform into an alcoholic beverage, people who attempt to walk on water always sink, and dead people stay dead) means that we always start out with powerful evidence that they do not happen. Therefore, we need especially convincing evidence in favor of a miracle story in order to be justified in believing it. But such evidence cannot be found. Instead, upon closer examination we can see that we have every reason to *doubt* the reliability of miracle stories and the people who tell them. Miracles are never witnessed by enough educated people, and stories of them typically originate from barbarous and unenlightened nations. In addition, reflection on human nature reveals that we love hearing and telling juicy stories, and we're inclined to believe them without bothering to think critically about the quality of evidence we have for them. (This human tendency explains how unfounded gossip gets passed around.) Not only that, but each religious tradition has its own miracle stories which effectively contradict the stories from every other tradition. Thus, Hume concludes, the evidence we have for miracle stories is always dubious and never sufficient to justify belief in them.

Theists respond in different ways to Hume's attack on belief in miracles. Hume, as you may have noticed, endorses **evidentialism**, and thus holds that beliefs must be based on evidence in order to be rational. Some theists agree with this, but argue in response to Hume that there is in fact solid historical evidence in support of certain miracle stories. Others, particularly **Reformed epistemologists**, reject evidentialism and argue that we can know that miracles like the resurrection happened on account of God's revelation to us that they did.

David Hume's classic essay, "Of Miracles," is found in his *An Enquiry Concerning Human Understanding*. His essay has spawned numerous books and articles. In *The Resurrection of God Incarnate* (Oxford: Oxford University Press, 2003), Richard Swinburne offers a critique of Hume's argument and a defense of belief in a particular miracle, the resurrection of Jesus.

Molinism

Molinism is a theory about **divine providence** named after Luis de Molina (1535–1600), the Spanish Jesuit priest who first put it into writing. The theory can be understood to take a middle ground between the more extreme positions of **Calvinism** and **open theism**. Calvinism takes a strong view of providence, affirming God's foreknowledge while denying that we have **libertarian freedom** (that is, freedom to do other than what we do, a kind of freedom that can only be had by agents whose actions are not causally determined by God or anything else). Open theism takes a weaker view of providence, affirming libertarian freedom while denying that God has comprehensive foreknowledge. Molinism attempts to find the middle ground, holding to divine foreknowledge and libertarian freedom at the same time. Here we'll find out how Molinists claim to toe this line, and then we'll look at a pair of objections to their view.

To understand Molinism, we first must understand the notion of *middle knowledge*, acceptance of which sets Molinism apart from Calvinism and open theism.

What is middle knowledge? It is knowledge of what are called *counterfactuals of creaturely freedom*, or just counterfactuals for short. (They are also sometimes called subjunctive conditionals.) Counterfactuals are statements about what some person *would* freely do under specific circumstances, often circumstances that don't in fact obtain. (Hence counterfactuals are "counter to fact.") Consider some important choice you have made in your life. Would you have made a different choice had the circumstances been different? It may help to give an example. Suppose you chose to attend Princeton University as an undergraduate. What would you have done had your application to Princeton been rejected? The proposition specifying what you would have done if that had happened is a counterfactual of creaturely freedom. Here is an example of such a counterfactual: *if Sally had been rejected by Princeton, she would have freely gone to Rutgers instead*. The key point here is that according to Molinism, such counterfactuals can be true. There are truths about what free choices you would have made in different circumstances, and there are also truths about what free choices you will make in situations in which you will eventually find yourself. Since God is **omniscient**, which means God knows every true proposition, God knows those truths as well.

We need to consider further the scope of these counterfactuals, to give some sense of what a vast storehouse of knowledge they contain. On Molinism, there are truths about what free choices you will make in circumstances you will eventually encounter (in which you will have a free choice to make), and truths about what free choices you would make in circumstances you won't encounter. In fact, there are true counterfactuals about what free choices you would make in *any possible circumstances* that you could be in. This is the case not just for you, but for every person in the world; and not just for every *created* person, but also for every *merely possible* person, that is, every person who God could have created but didn't. (Merely possible persons aren't really persons of course; it's just easier to talk about them that way. No doubt there are lots of merely possible persons, since God hasn't created all the people God could have.) It boggles the mind, then, to think about how many counterfactuals God must know—and pertaining to how many persons and how many circumstances. For any possible person and any possible situation in which that person could be left free with respect to some action, God knows what action that person would in fact freely choose to perform in that situation.

The next point to see is that the truth of these counterfactuals is *not up to God*. They are *contingent* truths, in that they could be different from what they are. (We are talking about libertarian freedom, after all, so that if people are free with respect to some action in some particular set of circumstances, it must be possible for them to perform that action and possible for them not to); but God does not determine which ones are true and which ones false. To see why this is so, return to the counterfactual we have already mentioned (varied slightly): *if Sally were rejected by Princeton, she would freely go to Rutgers*. The denial of that counterfactual is this one: *if Sally were rejected by Princeton, she would freely* not *go to Rutgers*. Molinists would say that one of those is true, and God knows which one. Now if God were to attempt to *make* one of those counterfactuals true by making it the case that Sally would perform one of those actions rather than the other, then Sally, if placed in those circumstances, would not be acting freely. God would be determining her choice, causing her to act as she does; and of course the Molinist, a proponent of libertarian freedom, thinks that such divine determination is incompatible with free choice. Thus in order for Sally's actions to be free, the truth value of those counterfactuals cannot be up to God.

The Molinist picture so far, then, is that God has middle knowledge, knowledge of which counterfactuals of creaturely freedom are true and which are false, where their truth or falsity is contingent but not under God's control. What's not so clear yet is why it's called *middle* knowledge—in the middle of what? Understanding this will enable us to see how middle knowledge helps God to decide how to set up the world and then to know exactly what will happen in it.

Molinists claim that there are three phases to God's knowledge, prior to creating the world. The first two together enable God to decide which world to create. The first phase is called God's *natural* knowledge. With this knowledge God knows all the possible ways things could be, or as we say in philosophy, all the **possible worlds**. God also knows, through this natural knowledge, all necessary truths, propositions which are true in *every* possible world. God knows, for example, that 2 + 2 = 4 in every possible world, because it is impossible for 2 + 2 to equal anything else. The number of possible worlds is unfathomably large, and God knows them all.

The second of the three phases of God's knowledge is, you guessed it, middle knowledge. In this phase God knows which counterfactuals of creaturely freedom are true—that is, which free choices all possible creatures would make in any situation in which they might be placed. And the key point here is this: in this phase God sees that there are many *possible* worlds that God is simply unable to create. Return to Sally and the college choice. If the choice is free, as we're supposing, then it would be possible in the circumstances where Princeton has turned her down for Sally to go to Rutgers, and possible for her not to. That is just to say that in some possible worlds, in those circumstances she freely goes to Rutgers, and in other possible worlds, in those circumstances she doesn't. Now Molinists affirm that some counterfactuals are true, and that there is a truth about what Sally *would* freely do in those circumstances. Suppose that she would in fact freely go to Rutgers. If that is true, then this fact serves to restrict the worlds that God can create. How? Because it means that God cannot create a world in which Sally is placed in exactly those circumstances and *doesn't* freely go to Rutgers.

This essential point can be generalized. With natural knowledge, God knows all possible worlds, but with middle knowledge, God knows which of those possible worlds God can create. All sorts of possible worlds are ruled out for God because of the free choices that creatures would actually make. If in fact a certain person would freely choose X if put in circumstances C, then there is nothing God can do about it. Again, Molinists believe that we have libertarian freedom, and a consequence of this is while God may know what free choices we are going to make (and what free choices we would make in other circumstances), what those choices are is up to us, and not up to God.

Still, God is by no means helpless on the Molinist picture. Having middle knowledge enables God to create a world where we are put in situations in which we make particular free choices (which God knew we would make) that altogether lead to a result where God's purposes are fulfilled. Thus following upon the second phase of knowledge comes what Molinists sometimes call "God's creative decision," where God decides which possible world to create or make actual. God decides, in other words, how things will go, where some of it will depend directly on God's action and some of it will depend on ours. Once this creative decision is made, the third phase of knowledge kicks in: God now has complete foreknowledge, knowledge of every situation that we will actually be placed in and of every free choice we will actually make.

That then is the complex but ingenious picture of divine providence that Molinists endorse. God exhibits a strong degree of sovereignty in creation by creating a world that fits with God's intentions and by knowing at all times everything that will happen in it; and yet God allows us libertarian freedom by giving us the power to make our own free choices and allowing us some say in the way that the world turns out. Not surprisingly, this picture has been the target of a number of objections, and here we shall briefly consider two of them.

The first objection is that the picture simply doesn't work, because foreknowledge and freedom are incompatible. Open theists press this objection, and indeed they reject divine foreknowledge largely on account of it. The gist of their argument is this: if God knows what we will do, then we can't do otherwise; and if we can't do otherwise, then we don't have free will. This powerful objection typically yields the following response from Molinists: God's knowing what choices we will make does not threaten the freedom of those choices because God's knowing doesn't *cause* us to choose that way. If anything, the causal dependence goes the other way: God knows we will make that choice *because* that is what we will choose. In this way Molinists insist that divine foreknowledge does not threaten our freedom.

The second objection is called the *grounding objection*. The Molinist picture, as we have seen, claims that God knows which counterfactuals are true before creating the world, and that this knowledge guides God's decision about which world to create. But the question is, in virtue of what are those counterfactuals true? What could make them true? What *grounds* their truth? Consider: on Molinism there were truths about what free choices you would make before you even existed, as well as truths about what free choices would be made by merely possible persons, persons who don't even exist.

It seems that such truths are, as we might say, free-floating, not attached to anything, not made true by anything. But there cannot *be* any such truths, the objection goes; all truths must be made true by *something*. If this is correct, and counterfactuals of creaturely freedom cannot be true, then God cannot have middle knowledge, and Molinism falls apart. Many of its critics have found this objection especially compelling, though Molinists have risen to respond to it and to the requirements for truth that it presupposes.

Thus Molinism represents a fascinating and controversial position in the debate over divine providence. It has important applications in other areas of philosophy of religion; in this book it is particularly relevant to the **free will defense**, which claims that God may be unable to create a world with freedom but no evil, even if such a world is in fact a possible one.

For an excellent explanation and defense of Molinism, see Thomas Flint, *Divine Providence: The Molinist Account* (Ithaca, NY: Cornell, 2006). For debate about Molinism and alternative views, where Molinism is defended by **William Lane Craig**, see *Divine Foreknowledge: Four Views*, eds. James Beilby and Paul Eddy (Downers Grove, IL: InterVarsity Press, 2001).

Moral argument

There are a number of moral arguments for belief in God. Here we'll look briefly at two such arguments and the challenge that they represent for non-theists. (For a third argument, see the one discussed under the **divine command theory** entry, courtesy of **Robert Merrihew Adams**.)

Some moral arguments for belief in God attempt to establish that God in fact exists. They do so by making the case that morality wouldn't be what it is if **atheism** were true. (See the **atheism** entry in this book for references to responses to this line of argument.) Our first argument, inspired by George Mavrodes (b. 1926), follows this pattern by focusing on the demanding nature of moral obligations. Morality requires much of us, including in some cases genuine self-sacrifice. In some situations we have the obligation to sacrifice our own interests, our well-being, or even our lives in service to others. Now, in a world where there is no God and where all that exists is matter in motion, such self-sacrifice is not ultimately beneficial to those engaged in it, mainly because there is no afterlife in which they might be rewarded. But this raises an important question: Where could these moral obligations come from in such a world? How could we even have them? It may not be surprising in a godless world for people to *believe* that they have moral obligations, since beliefs of that kind can promote the sort of selfless behavior that helps a group to survive over time; but it would be quite crazy for there actually to *be* such costly obligations with no possibility of reward. Yet such moral obligations do exist—we actually have them, and don't merely (falsely) believe that we do. As Mavrodes argues, their existence makes little sense in a godless world, and makes much more sense in a world where God exists and is the source of the moral law. That gives us good reason to think that this is not a godless world, and that God in fact exists.

Unlike the first, the second moral argument is a **pragmatic argument for belief in God**, based on one by **Immanuel Kant** (1724–1804). As a pragmatic argument, it doesn't provide evidence that God exists, but instead identifies desirable consequences of belief in God and encourages belief because of them. The consequences in this case are benefits to a person's moral life. Someone who sees that bad people often prosper and believes that there is no God to ultimately ensure that justice is done could on that account become disillusioned and lose motivation for behaving morally. That would be a bad thing. But belief in God, a being who is perfectly good and who promotes moral order by ensuring that moral behavior is rewarded and immoral behavior punished, can encourage moral living. In short, atheism can be demoralizing where **theism** is not, and this provides good practical reason for accepting theism.

Are these arguments compelling? For the first, does morality really have those features, and is it the case that theism can best account for them? For the second, do sociological studies support the contention that belief in God promotes moral behavior? These arguments and numerous variations on them continue to be hot topics in philosophy of religion. A popular presentation of a moral argument for God's existence can be found in Book I of **C. S. Lewis's** *Mere Christianity* (San Francisco: HarperSanFrancisco, 2001 [1952]). Mavrodes' influential paper is called "Religion and the Queerness of Morality" from *Rationality, Religious Belief and Moral Commitment*, Robert Audi and William J. Wainwright, eds. (Ithaca, NY: Cornell University Press, 1986). A version of Kant's pragmatic argument is found in Robert Adams, "Moral Arguments for Theistic Belief," in *Rationality and Religious Belief*, C. F. Delaney, ed. (Notre Dame: Notre Dame Press, 1977).

Naturalism

Naturalism is simply the view that the natural world is all that there is, and that there exist no gods or supernatural beings. A naturalist in this sense will also endorse **atheism**, but an atheist, committed only to denying the existence of the God of **theism**, could nonetheless affirm the existence of other supernatural realities and hence not be a naturalist. Still, many atheists are naturalists, particularly in the West; and the terms "atheism" and "naturalism" are sometimes used synonymously.

It is important to distinguish two varieties of naturalism. The first, which we can call *metaphysical naturalism*, endorses naturalism as just described. A metaphysical naturalist believes that there are no gods or supernatural beings. A second variety, *methodological naturalism*, is the view that when doing work in the sciences, we ought to operate as though metaphysical naturalism is true. In other words, methodological naturalism claims that scientific explanations of phenomena may not appeal to the supernatural. Methodological naturalism thus runs contrary to the stance of the **intelligent design** movement, which maintains that certain features of the natural world cannot be explained without appeal to the supernatural, to something or someone outside of the natural realm. One can be a methodological naturalist without being a metaphysical naturalist: many religious believers who aren't metaphysical naturalists nonetheless believe that the ground rules for scientific research require that supernatural explanations of natural phenomena be kept out of play. Whether they are correct on this point is a matter of considerable debate among those who ponder the relation between **religion and science**.

Naturalism is a common viewpoint in contemporary philosophy and philosophy of religion. It is also the target of the **evolutionary argument against naturalism**, which attempts to establish that if naturalism is true and we were produced by the process described in the **theory of evolution**, it is very unlikely that we are able to come to true beliefs about the world, and hence that everyone who accepts naturalism and evolution should be skeptical about all of their beliefs, including their belief in those theories.

Natural law

Natural law is a notion developed by **Thomas Aquinas** (1225–74) that is central to the natural law tradition in ethics. The basic idea is this. All natural things, Aquinas says, have a *telos*, an end or goal at which they aim. (Here Aquinas, as he often does, is borrowing from **Aristotle** (384–322 B.C.E.), who referred to the *telos* of a natural thing as its final cause.) Human beings are natural things, so we have a *telos* as well. Our *telos* is happiness—not mere contentment, but a richer kind of happiness that involves flourishing as a human being—and we by nature are inclined to pursue it. To achieve happiness we must follow natural law, the law of human nature, which can be understood by reason and which dictates in general terms how we must behave if we are to flourish. This law states, for example, that we must pursue good and avoid evil; we must produce and preserve life; we must educate ourselves and our children; and we must live in community. To do otherwise is to behave unnaturally, to go against our nature. Since natural law is accessible to reason, it doesn't need to be divinely revealed to us; people who go wrong on matters of religious faith can nonetheless discern the basic outline of how they must behave in order to flourish.

How is natural law connected with ethics? In short, natural law on this understanding underlies the moral law, so that what is morally right is what naturally contributes to the fulfillment of our *telos*, while what is wrong is what is fundamentally unnatural and damaging to us. This conception of morality and its connection with human nature is at the heart of the natural law tradition in ethics, a tradition that is particularly influential in the moral reasoning of the Roman Catholic Church.

Natural law theory is often opposed to **divine command theory**, in so far as it offers an opposing solution to the **Euthyphro problem**. While divine command theory asserts that right actions are right because God commands them, natural law theory states that God commands actions because they are right, and they are right in so far as they cohere with natural law and therefore contribute to our fulfilling our purpose as human beings. For more on this debate, see the Janine Marie Idziak and Craig A. Boyd / Raymond

VanArragon exchange in *Contemporary Debates in Philosophy of Religion*, Michael Peterson and Raymond VanArragon, eds. (New York: Blackwell, 2003), 290–314. For Aquinas's brilliant discussion of natural law, see his *Treatise on Law*, Richard J. Regan, trans. (Indianapolis: Hackett, 2000), which is excerpted from the second part of his **Summa Theologica**.

Natural theology

Natural theology is the field of study that aims to prove the existence of God by way of arguments that any rational person might find compelling. The proofs for God's existence discussed in this book all constitute examples of natural theology, including the **cosmological argument**, the **kalam cosmological argument**, the **ontological argument**, and the **teleological argument**. These arguments appeal only to premises derived from rational reflection and/or observation, and not to divine revelation, in order to establish their conclusions. Theists who accept **evidentialism**, the view that all rational belief must be supported by evidence, are likely to place a high premium on natural theology, since evidentialism implies that the rationality of belief in God depends on its success.

Negative theology

Negative theology (also called *apophatic* theology) states that our concepts simply cannot apply to God, and that the best we can do in describing God is to take what's called the *via negativa* (the "negative way") and say what God is not. Negative theology thus differs from the view which says that our concepts literally apply to God, and from the view, called the theory of **analogy**, which claims that our concepts apply to God analogically. The intuitive idea behind negative theology is that an infinite God is so far beyond us that we cannot begin to fathom what such a God is like. One notable proponent of negative theology was the medieval Jewish philosopher Miamonides (1138–1204), who defended it in his book *Guide of the Perplexed*. Besides endorsing the intuitive idea behind the theory, Miamonides also labeled as demeaning to God the notion that God's attributes are somehow like ours.

While negative theology is a theory specifically about how our concepts apply to God, other non-theistic religions, including Buddhism and Hinduism, have been similarly hesitant to suggest that we can make positive claims about the divine reality. An example of this can be seen in an important text from the Taoist religion, the *Tao Te Ching*. The book's opening lines, published in a number of philosophy of religion anthologies, indicate how the Tao cannot be described by human language.

Omnipotence

Omnipotence is the characteristic of being all-powerful. To be all-powerful means to be capable of doing anything (with qualifications that we'll discuss in a moment). According to classical **theism**, omnipotence is one of God's primary attributes, together with **omniscience** and **perfect goodness**. We'll investigate further what omnipotence means, and then consider some potential problems with it.

What does it mean to be omnipotent? It might be helpful to answer this question by distinguishing between actions an omnipotent being can and cannot perform. Most philosophers think that an omnipotent being can part the Red Sea and change water into wine. (Christians typically believe that God *has* done those things.) Those actions are **miracles**, and as such they violate the laws of nature; but violating those laws wouldn't be a problem for an omnipotent being. However, most philosophers do not think that an omnipotent being could make 2+2=17, or make a triangle with four sides, or make a contradiction true. It is *logically impossible* to perform such feats, and being omnipotent doesn't mean being capable of doing what is logically impossible. Having the power to make a four-sided triangle isn't really a power anyway, when you stop to think about it. The very notion of such a triangle simply doesn't make any sense. Neither would it make any sense for two plus two to equal anything other than four. (Of course we could use different *words* to express the truth that 2+2=4, but that wouldn't change the truth that we were expressing. Nothing could change the fact that 2+2=4; in the strongest sense it simply *must* be true. It is a *necessary* truth; and even an omnipotent being couldn't change one of those.) So an omnipotent being's power is limited by the rules of logic; but these aren't limits that should bother anyone.

Some philosophers have argued that it is impossible for a being to be omnipotent. If this argument is successful, that would effectively prove that God does not exist since, as we've said, omnipotence is supposed to be one of God's essential attributes. One version of this argument comes in the form of a puzzle about omnipotence, known as the *paradox of the stone*. The puzzle takes the form of a question.

Can an omnipotent being create a stone so heavy he can't lift it?

Perhaps you can see the problem that the question poses. If we say, yes, an omnipotent being *can* create such a stone, we are granting that there is something the being cannot do, namely, lift a stone it could create, in which case it is not omnipotent. On the other hand, if we say, no, an omnipotent being *cannot* create such a stone, then again we are granting that there is something it cannot do, namely, create such a stone—in which case, again, it is not omnipotent. Since the answer to our question must be yes or no, and either one yields the conclusion that our being isn't omnipotent after all, it follows that it is impossible for a being to be omnipotent. And if that is so, then God, as conceived by classical theism, does not exist.

But we already have available the resources to give the standard reply to this argument. An omnipotent being cannot perform the logically impossible, we said. Would either of the options presented in the previous paragraph be logically impossible? Indeed, one would: it seems that it would be logically impossible for there to be a stone so heavy that an omnipotent being couldn't lift it. An omnipotent being could lift any stone that could be made. (Pick any weight; an omnipotent being could lift it. Add a few pounds; he could still lift it . . .) Thus the answer to the question should be this: No, an omnipotent being cannot create such a stone, since doing so would be logically impossible. But since omnipotence doesn't require the ability to do the logically impossible, it follows that this inability does not threaten a being's omnipotence. The possibility of an omnipotent being, and the possibility of God's existing, is preserved.

One final problem we should raise about omnipotence, particularly as it applies to God. According to classical theism, as we have said, God is omnipotent, omniscient, and perfectly good. Let's focus on omnipotence and perfect goodness. Can God possibly have both of these attributes? The worry here is that God's goodness might restrict God's power in such a way that there are logically possible things that God cannot do, because they'd be wrong. Let's consider an outlandish example of an action that an omnipotent being could perform but, one thinks, God can't. Suppose we took all of the world's most morally upright people, together with all sorts of innocents (particularly young children), plunked them in a large frying pan at high temperature, and left them there for a good long time. This action would be morally heinous, and thus God, being perfectly good, can't perform it. And yet a malevolent omnipotent being (hopefully there is no such being!)

could do it with no trouble at all. Thus there are some logically possible actions that God cannot do. But then God's perfect goodness prevents God from being omnipotent!

Or does it? There are a number of ways that theists have responded to this problem, but one way has been to distinguish between actions that God has the *power* to perform, and actions God's moral character permits God to perform. There are no doubt morally reprehensible actions that *you* are physically able to perform (you have the physical tools, so to speak), but your moral virtue prevents you. Perhaps we should say that your character doesn't eliminate your powers; it just controls their usage. And maybe the same applies to God. God is omnipotent (all-powerful), but God's goodness limits the way that God's power can be used.

For more discussion of omnipotence and some puzzles that attend it, see Thomas V. Morris, *Our Idea of God* (Vancouver: Regent College Publishing, 1997).

Omniscience

According to classical **theism**, omniscience is one of God's essential attributes, together with **omnipotence** and **perfect goodness**. To say that God is omniscient is to say that God is all-knowing, which means that for any true proposition or statement, God knows that that proposition is true. (When you start thinking about all the truths there are, including truths about mathematics and physics, the past, present, and maybe the future, you can begin to glimpse how mind-boggling an attribute omniscience is.)

There are numerous puzzles surrounding omniscience, but perhaps the most troubling has to do with **free will**. If God knows all truths, the thinking goes, then God knows what will happen in the future. But if God knows, for example, that exactly twenty years from this moment you will order a Big Mac at McDonald's, then how can you do anything other than that? And if you cannot do anything other than order a Big Mac, how can your ordering it constitute a free action? And if God always knows *everything* that you are going to do, well, how can you have free will at all? In short, God's foreknowledge seems to lock the future in place and threaten our freedom. **Calvinism**, **Molinism**, and **open theism** constitute attempts to solve this problem and reconcile divine omniscience and human free will.

For a classic statement of the problem, see Nelson Pike, "Divine Omniscience and Voluntary Action," *The Philosophical Review* 74 (1965), 27–46, reprinted in many anthologies.

Ontological argument

The ontological argument is a famous and controversial argument that essentially starts with the definition of God as the greatest possible being and infers from it that God must exist. It differs from other arguments for God's existence in virtue of its being an *a priori* argument, the sort of argument you could come up with while sitting in an easy chair, without going out and observing anything. (The **cosmological** and **teleological arguments**, on the other hand, both appeal to observed facts about the natural world and hence are known as *a posteriori* arguments.)

Several versions of the ontological argument have been paraded out over the years. In what follows we'll consider a version which was spelled out by William Rowe (b. 1931), who based it on the argument found in the book **Proslogium**, by **St. Anselm** (1033–1109). We'll see how the argument goes, and then we'll consider a couple of objections to it.

As we said, in the argument we'll define "God" as "the greatest possible being." (Anselm used the phrase "that than which none greater can be conceived," but "greatest possible being" is simpler.) Note that giving this definition does not involve assuming that God actually exists. We can define "unicorn" as "magical horse with horn" without assuming that unicorns actually exist. Note also that a greatest *possible* something is different from a greatest *actual* something. Tiger Woods is the greatest actual golfer, but he's not the greatest possible golfer. There is no one in the world better at golf than him, but there *could* be. The greatest possible golfer would presumably achieve a hole-in-one on every hole; it would be impossible to do better than that.

Here, then, is the first premise of the argument.

1. God exists in the understanding.

Anselm means nothing controversial by this premise. To exist in the understanding is merely to exist as an object of thought. If we can think about God,
the greatest possible being, then God exists in the understanding. And clearly
we *can* think about God. Even **atheists** can think about God, as evidenced by
their belief that God does not exist in *reality*. The mere fact that they have this
belief means that God exists in the understanding—their understanding.

Before continuing, we need to highlight the distinction we've just drawn
between *existing in the understanding* and *existing in reality*, because it is
very important to the rest of the argument. Anselm's own example to illustrate the distinction is a painting which only exists in the artist's understanding
up until it is actually painted, at which point it exists both in the artist's understanding and in reality. We can come up with other examples. Santa Claus
exists only in the understanding but not in reality. Ditto for Sherlock Holmes,
the tooth fairy, and Hermione Granger. On the other hand, former U.S. presi-
dents Bill Clinton and George W. Bush exist both in the understanding and
in reality. We can think about them, and they are actually out there in the
world somewhere, engaging in their post-presidential activities. Santa Claus,
on the other hand, isn't out there at all. He exists only in the understanding,
and not in reality.

Premise (1) of the argument, then, says that God exists in the understanding;
the point of the argument, however, is to prove that God also exists in reality.

Here is the second premise:

2. God could possibly exist in reality.

This needs some explaining. Note that the second premise doesn't say that
God *does* exist in reality; it simply says that God *could* exist in reality. It claims,
in other words, that there is nothing impossible about a greatest possible
being existing in reality. To understand this point a little better we should
consider some things that only exist in the understanding but could exist in
reality, and compare them with things that only exist in the understanding but
could *not* exist in reality.

Santa Claus, we have said, exists only in the understanding; but surely he could exist in reality. There could be a portly gentleman who rides around in his sleigh on Christmas Eve delivering toys to the good boys and girls throughout the world. In general, lots of things that exist merely in thought could also exist in reality (or could have at some point in time), even though they don't.

On the other hand, some things we can think about are *impossible*, which means that even though they exist in the understanding, they simply couldn't exist in reality. Consider a square-circle. We can think about it and even define it. A square-circle is a two-dimensional four-sided figure, all of whose points are equidistant from the center. We know that something like *that* couldn't exist in reality. Consider also the greatest possible natural number, the number such that no number can be greater than it. We can think about such a thing, which means it exists in the understanding; but we also recognize upon reflection that a greatest possible natural number couldn't possibly exist in reality. Why not? Well, for any candidate greatest possible number, no matter how mind-bogglingly high, we can always get a greater one simply by adding one more to it. Like a square-circle, the greatest possible natural number exists in the understanding but couldn't possibly exist in reality.

Again, our second premise tells us that God, like Santa but unlike a square-circle or the greatest possible natural number, could possibly exist in reality.

The third premise follows:

3. If something exists only in the understanding and could possibly exist in reality, then it could possibly be greater than it is.

This premise is meant to make a general claim about existence in the understanding versus existence in reality. We can understand it best by using an example. Suppose that your friend is going to set you up on a date, and describes the person to you as follows: "Marissa is a fantastic person. She is highly intelligent, a splendid conversationalist, good looking, athletic; she is enormously talented and accomplished; she shares your religious and political beliefs; and besides all that she is especially attracted to people just like you. There's only one catch: [dramatic pause] Marissa exists only in the understanding, and not in reality." Chances are you'd be disappointed, and you might blurt out, "Marissa would be a lot greater if she existed in reality!" That's exactly the point of premise (3). Anything that exists only in the understanding but could possibly exist in reality (surely it is possible for there to be a person like Marissa) could be greater than it is—that is, if it existed in reality, too. Existing in reality makes a thing greater than it otherwise would be, so anything that could exist in reality but doesn't could be greater than it is.

It is very important to note here that if you have accepted the first three premises of this argument, then you are well on the way to accepting that God does in fact exist in reality. The first three premises do all the work; and, as we'll see, it is a very short step from them to the desired conclusion.

On then to the fourth premise.

4. Suppose God exists only in the understanding.

With this premise, Anselm is trying to set us up. He is employing an argument form known as a *reductio ad absurdum*, which means that he is assuming the *negation* of what he is trying to prove, and will try to show that a contradiction follows from that assumption. If he can show that, then he will have proven that the assumption in this premise is false, and that God must exist in reality.

Perhaps you can anticipate how things will go from here, just by thinking through the premises already stated. Given that (4) is true, and together with (2) and (3), we get this:

5. God could possibly have been greater than God is.

That is, if God exists only in the understanding, but could exist in reality (as (2) says), then God could be greater than God is. And now we have a problem. For it follows from (5) that

6. God is not the greatest possible being,

which, given our definition of "God," is just to say that

7. The greatest possible being is not the greatest possible being.

And that is about as clear a contradiction as you'll ever see. So, since our assumption in (4) led us straight into a contradiction, that assumption must be mistaken. We'll make that the next premise, which is sort of a sub-conclusion:

8. It is false that God exists only in the understanding.

And since, as (1) tells us, God does exist in the understanding, it follows that

9. God exists in reality.

This is exactly what we were trying to prove.

That, then, is one way of understanding Anselm's ontological argument. The basic idea of the argument—that a greatest possible being must exist in reality, since if it didn't then it wouldn't be the greatest possible being—is ingenious, yet few who have encountered the argument have been persuaded by it. Most people tend to think that there has to be something wrong with it; but where is the mistake?

We'll look at two objections. The most famous objection, put forward by a contemporary of Anselm named Gaunilo, claims that there must be *something* wrong with the argument because precisely parallel arguments can be put forward for all sorts of obviously false conclusions. If so, then we know that such arguments cannot be trusted, even if we can't determine exactly what's wrong with them.

What sorts of parallel arguments did Gaunilo propose? He suggested that we could use a sort of ontological argument to prove the existence of the "greatest possible island." Just substitute "greatest possible island" for "greatest possible being" in the argument above, and proceed as before. Such an island exists in the understanding and could exist in reality. And if we suppose that it only exists in the understanding, we run into a similar contradiction: the greatest possible island is not the greatest possible island. So then the greatest possible island must exist in reality! Indeed, we can repeat this reasoning for the greatest possible fill-in-the-blank, and prove the existence of such wonders as the greatest possible strawberry pie, greatest possible cross country runner, and even the greatest possible manure pile! The key to Gaunilo's objection is that while these arguments can "prove" the existence of these things, obviously these "greatest possible" things do not in fact exist in reality. (There may be a greatest *actual* cross country runner, but recall our point above that there's a huge difference between being the greatest actual and the greatest *possible* something-or-other.) So, since these parallel arguments prove all sorts of obviously false conclusions, they cannot be trusted—and neither can the ontological argument.

A second objection to the argument applies to premise (2), which asserts that God, the greatest possible being, could possibly exist in reality. What reason do we have for thinking that that is true? There are certainly reasons for doubting it, including one that falls right out of our earlier discussion of the premise. We noted there that the greatest possible natural number is something that exists in the understanding (we can think about it) but couldn't possibly exist in reality, because for any natural number we pick, we could get a greater one simply by adding to it. But why think a greatest possible *being* is any different? Maybe a greatest possible being is impossible simply because for any great being you pick, there could always be a greater one. In other words, maybe beings are like the natural numbers—there can't be a greatest possible. How can we establish that a greatest possible being really could exist in reality? A person who doubted this could sensibly doubt the whole argument, since the argument doesn't go anywhere without premise (2). For the argument to succeed it seems that more evidence should be provided for the claim that God could possibly exist in reality; and it is not clear what sort of evidence for this there might be.

Additional objections to the ontological argument have been posed as well, particularly by **Immanuel Kant** (1724–1804) who claimed that it fails because "existence is not a predicate"—it isn't a property that can be added to a thing that doesn't already have it. (We can add the property "redness" to a chair by painting it red, but we can't in the same way add "existence" to it. If we are adding any properties to the chair, it must already have existence!) If we translate "existence" here to mean "existence in reality," we can understand Kant as questioning our use of that notion and its supposed counterpart, "existence in the understanding." Is it correct to suggest, as Anselm does, that a painting first exists in the understanding and then has the property of "existence in reality" added to it when the painter does her work? Readers are encouraged to ponder further the use our argument makes of these two "kinds" of existing, to see whether it holds up. We should repeat, however, that there are many different versions of the ontological argument; and some have been formulated to avoid Kant's objection.

For further development and critique of the argument discussed here, see the third chapter of William Rowe's *Philosophy of Religion: An Introduction* 4th ed. (Belmont, CA: Wadsworth, 2007). For discussion and critique of different versions of the argument, including the so-called *modal version*, see chapter 6 of Peter van Inwagen's, *Metaphysics* 3rd ed. (Boulder, CO: Westview, 2008).

Open theism

Open theism is a position in the debate over the nature of **divine providence**, a position that takes the dramatic step of denying that God has comprehensive foreknowledge. Open theism constitutes a recent, controversial, but increasingly popular entry in the field. Many theists reject it, thinking that it strays too far from the view of God embraced in centuries past. But its proponents believe that only open theism can make room for genuine **free will** and moral responsibility, and argue that any compromises made regarding God's sovereignty are entirely acceptable.

To understand open theism, the first thing to see is that open theists accept a **libertarian** account of free will: they believe that freedom requires the ability to do otherwise, and that freedom is incompatible with **determinism**. They believe, moreover, that we *have* this type of freedom. Thus far open theism differs from **Calvinism** but agrees with **Molinism**. It parts ways with Molinism, however, in claiming that libertarian free will is incompatible with divine foreknowledge. If God knows what you will do in the future, open theists argue, then you cannot do anything other than that. You cannot make God wrong, after all. Divine foreknowledge locks the future in place, depriving us of the ability to do otherwise and hence depriving us of freedom. Thus, open theists reason, since we have libertarian freedom it must be that God does not have comprehensive foreknowledge.

On the face of it, rejecting divine foreknowledge seems to mean rejecting divine **omniscience**; and this would be a deeply problematic implication if it were correct. Yet open theists claim to embrace the notion that God is omniscient. How can they do so? How can God be omniscient if God doesn't know what will happen in the future?

Open theists typically respond to this question as follows. To be omniscient, on the traditional account, is to know all truths. That is, if God exists, then for any true statement or proposition (we'll treat "statements" and "propositions" as synonyms), God knows that it is true. Consider a proposition about a free future action that someone, Martha, will perform: *On September 22, 2028, Martha will choose to have pepperoni pizza for dinner*. If that proposition is true, then God must know that it is. Open theists, of course, deny that God knows that it's true; but this does not present a problem for omniscience on their view because they also deny that the proposition *is* true. Indeed, they deny the truth of the following proposition as well: *On September 22, 2028, Martha will choose* not *to have pepperoni pizza for dinner*. God can be omniscient despite not knowing which of them is true—because neither one is! This point can be generalized: propositions about so-called future contingents (that is, about events in the future that will not *necessarily* happen) are not true at all, and hence God's failure to know them and consequent failure to know what will happen in the future does not threaten God's omniscience.

That seems like a good way to preserve omniscience while denying foreknowledge, but do we have any good, independent reason for thinking that propositions about future contingents really are not true? According to open theists, we do. Consider this. For any proposition to be true, something in the world has to *make* it true. That seems like common sense. The proposition that *there's a refrigerator in your house* is made true by the existence of the refrigerator and its placement in your house. If there were no refrigerator to make that proposition true, it wouldn't *be* true. But here's the problem with propositions about future contingents: what is there that can make them true? Consider Martha and the pepperoni pizza. What about the world right now makes it the case that she will eat the pizza in 2028, or that she won't? Open theists argue that nothing does, and nothing could. The future isn't real yet; it doesn't exist to make true the statements that attempt to describe it. There is nothing about the present that guarantees that Martha will make that choice in 2028 (or for that matter that she'll even be alive in 2028); and indeed, if that choice *were* guaranteed, then it wouldn't be free since she wouldn't be able to choose differently. Thus, according to open theists, the future really is *open*—what it holds is to a considerable degree up in the air—which means that propositions about what is going to happen aren't true. (Note: God knows *necessary* truths about the future: in the future, triangles will continue to have three sides, 2 + 2 will equal 4, and God will still be good. God knows that; God just doesn't know truths about future contingents, because there are no such truths.)

On open theism, then, we are left with an omniscient but foreknowledge-lacking God, and an open future. But this God, while lacking the degree of providential control that Calvinists ascribe to God, still has the power and resources to ensure that things work out roughly according to plan. After all, at every moment God's own plans are set; God knows every possible outcome that can result from people's free choices (even though God doesn't know for sure which choices will be made or which outcomes will result); God also knows what people are *likely* to choose; and moreover God is capable of intervening at any moment in case events start to go badly off track. So while it is true that God is a risk-taker and God's specific ways of working out God's plan constantly fluctuate depending on the choices people make, we can be assured that God will ultimately triumph over evil and that God's intentions for this world will be worked out in glorious fashion.

That is the picture of divine providence that open theism presents. Not surprisingly, there are powerful objections to open theism, and here we'll consider two of them. The first is that not only does lacking foreknowledge seem like a fairly serious deficiency for the God of theism, but it also seems to run contrary to accounts of prophecy found in the different theistic religious traditions. In the Christian New Testament, for example, Jesus prophesies that his disciple Peter will deny him that night (the night Jesus was arrested) three times before the rooster crows (see Matthew 24:34 and 26:69–75). If open theism is true, how could Jesus have known that Peter was going to do that? (How could Jesus have even known that Peter would find himself in that situation in the first place?) We wouldn't want to say that Jesus simply made a good guess. We might also be hesitant to say Jesus made the prediction and that God stood by ready to compel the relevant people to behave accordingly. In short, as the issue of prophesy illustrates, open theists need to square their denial of foreknowledge with claims from their traditions that seems to conflict with it.

The second objection goes back to the suggestion that lacking foreknowledge doesn't threaten God's omniscience, because statements about future contingents aren't true. The problem is that this suggestion runs contrary to the way we usually think about such statements. Suppose you say in April, "The Yankees will win the World Series this year!" and lo and behold that October (or these days November) the Yankees do in fact win. The rest of us, remembering your prediction, will be inclined to think that what you said in April was true, and it was true when you said it (even if you and the rest of us didn't know it at the time). But open theists seem committed to saying that what you said wasn't true. That seems a little strange. (It also opens the door to additional puzzles. If what you said wasn't true, was it *false*? But how can that be if the Yankees ended up winning the World Series? And if what you said wasn't true *or* false, what exactly was it?) And if a theory has strange consequences, that can call into question the viability of the theory itself.

Fortunately, much has been written in recent years exploring, defending, and criticizing open theism, so readers are invited to read further to pursue these and other objections to the theory. For a thorough defense from a Christian perspective, see Robert Rice et al., *The Openness of God* (Downers Grove, IL: InterVarsity Press, 1994). For debate about it and presentation of some alternative views, see *Divine Foreknowledge: Four Views*, eds. James Beilby and Paul Eddy (Downers Grove, IL: InterVarsity Press, 2001).

Pascal's Wager

Pascal's Wager is a **pragmatic argument for belief in God**—an argument not that God exists, but that we should for pragmatic reasons *believe* in God. It is named for Blaise Pascal (1623–62), a brilliant French mathematician and philosopher who came up with a famous version of the wager, published in his book **Pensees**. Pascal was opposed to **evidentialism**, the view that we must have good evidence for all of our beliefs. He thought that the evidence for or against God's existence was bound to be insufficient, given our finitude and God's comparative greatness. But, he argued, we still have to make a choice whether to (a) believe in God, or (b) not believe in God. What should we do?

Pascal recommends, in effect, that we approach this choice like gamblers. We should decide where to place our bets, given the potential consequences of each option. We can't be sure which consequences will obtain, because that depends on whether God exists. But let's think through the possibilities. If we take option (a) and God *does* exist, then the outcome will be rosy for us indeed: we'll end up in heaven, enjoying endless communion with God. If we take (a) and God does *not* exist, well, then we will live a believer's life with its hardships and challenges, but when we die, that's the end. We won't even find out we were wrong! If instead we take option (b) and God doesn't exist, we will live an unbeliever's life and that will be it; but if we take (b) and God does exist, we are in a world of trouble. We won't get eternal joy; instead we'll get eternal suffering in **hell**. That's not an appealing outcome! (Note that it's also not an outcome that was included as part of Pascal's original wager. Many popular accounts of the wager add the hell outcome, but the argument works fine without it, provided we stipulate that only belief in God can yield eternal bliss. Here we've added the hell possibility just to make the choice clearer.)

So, believing can lead to eternal bliss, and the worst consequence it can yield is a difficult earthly life (and maybe not even that—Pascal claims that the life of a believer is better even if God doesn't exist); while not believing can lead to eternal misery, and at best whatever goods can be gained during the earthly life of an unbeliever. But then it's an easy choice: we should believe. In our current condition, where the evidence for and against God's existence can't settle the matter, we've got to place a bet, and believing in God is the only sensible bet to make.

That's Pascal's Wager, an argument remarkable for its power and simplicity. When the choice is laid out so starkly, it seems like a no-brainer. But there are objections, and we'll talk about three of them, one friendly and two not. The first objection is the friendly one. Suppose you have followed Pascal's argument and decided that you should believe in God. The problem is that up to now you *haven't* believed in God; and it's not as if you can simply flip a switch and turn on belief. (Try it: consider something you don't believe at the moment, and decide to believe it. Decide to believe, for example, that the political party you have always opposed is actually right about pretty much everything. Chances are, you can't do it. We just don't have that sort of control over what we believe.) So then how can you make the wager Pascal has recommended? Fortunately, he has a solution to this conundrum, and it's essentially this: you should hang out with believers and do what they do. Read what they read, listen to what they listen to; in short, act like you believe, and eventually you will! And whatever benefits they acquire from believing, you will acquire, too.

The next two objections are less friendly. First, there seems to be something wrong with this whole approach to religious belief, where you are encouraged to believe because of the potential reward of doing so. One might wonder whether God would look favorably on those who come to believe in this way. Second, the belief options that we have are not really as simple as Pascal's Wager makes them out to be. Our choice is not simply, "Believe in God, or not"; instead, there are all sorts of religions out there, theistic and otherwise, and we have to choose one. Suppose that some of these religions claim that only adherents to their religion will achieve salvation and all others will suffer eternally in hell. Then any choice we make has the possible consequence of eternal bliss—which we'll achieve if the religion we pick is the right one—but also the possible consequence of eternal suffering—which we'll get if we choose wrongly and one of those other religions is correct. What guidance can Pascal's Wager give us in such a complicated religious arena?

Thus, Pascal's Wager has been the source of much interest and discussion. Readers are invited to explore it further by consulting Jeff Jordan, *Pascal's Wager: Pragmatic Arguments and Belief in God* (New York: Oxford, 2006).

Perfect goodness

Perfect goodness is one of God's essential attributes, according to classical **theism** (together with **omnipotence** and **omniscience**). To say that God is perfectly good is to say that God has ultimate value as a being and that God is morally perfect. To say that this is one of God's *essential* attributes means that it is impossible for God *not* to be perfectly good. God literally cannot do wrong.

There are puzzles connected with this notion of perfect goodness, and we'll briefly mention two of them. First, many philosophers have used the **problem of evil** as an argument against God's goodness (no perfectly good being would allow so much evil that it could prevent), and hence against God's existence (since any being that is not perfectly good is not God). Second, we might wonder why believers *praise* God for God's actions if, as we just said, God simply cannot do wrong. We praise people for doing what's right when we think that they could have done wrong and perhaps were strongly tempted to do so. But nothing similar seems to apply to a being that has perfect goodness as an essential attribute. So, while theists should no doubt be happy that God is perfectly good, further reflection on the nature of that goodness raises questions about how the praise believers direct toward God can be merited.

For further reading on divine goodness, see Thomas V. Morris, *Our Idea of God* (Vancouver: Regent College Publishing, 1997).

Petitionary prayer

Engaging in petitionary prayer is a common practice among theists, but reflection can lead us to question the point of it. In short, petitionary prayer involves asking God to do something; but does such prayer make any difference to what God actually does?

It is pretty clear that praying can have benefits for the person doing it. A person who asks God for help in her own life may feel comforted upon doing so. One who makes a habit of praying for others will likely feel more empathy and concern for them, which is all to the good. There may also be benefits to those who are prayed for, in so far as knowing that they are prayed for may give them hope. (Recent studies have raised questions about whether this sort of petitionary prayer—called intercessory prayer—consistently has such benefits, but it probably has them some of the time.)

But there are reasons for thinking that God would not be affected by petitionary prayer. Suppose that you pray that your Aunt Suzy might recover from some illness. No doubt God already knows Aunt Suzy's condition, and knows the consequences of intervening and of not intervening. Moreover, God is perfectly good and loving, and hence wants what is best for everyone involved in the situation. One thinks, then, that if God sees that healing Aunt Suzy would be for the best, then God would do so. Why would your *asking* make any difference? And if it does make a difference, so that God heals Aunt Suzy on account of your praying and wouldn't do so if you didn't, what does that mean for those less fortunate people who don't have anyone to pray for them? Are they just left to suffer? That would hardly seem fair.

Thus the practice of petitionary prayer presents philosophical problems. Because of them, some theists have concluded that indeed God does not respond to prayer, and that petitionary prayer benefits only those doing the praying (and perhaps those who know they are prayed for). But others have argued that God could have good reason for responding to such prayers and failing to act in their absence. They have argued, in other words, that petitionary prayer may have an effect on how God acts in the world.

What reason could there be? Eleonore Stump (b. 1946) suggests that by answering petitionary prayer God might prevent certain kinds of problems from cropping up in the divine-human relationship. That relationship is remarkably lopsided, after all, with God being so much more powerful and knowledgeable than we are. If God were to fulfill our needs without waiting for us to ask, that could result in our becoming either spoiled (like the cronies of a mafia boss) or overwhelmed (like children of dominating parents). To prevent this, God follows a policy of sometimes fulfilling our needs *because* we ask, and waiting until we ask to fulfill them.

This is only the beginning of an account of why God might respond to petitionary prayer—it doesn't yet explain why God might not help *other* people unless we pray for them. For further development of this account, see Stump's essay, "Petitionary Prayer," *American Philosophical Quarterly* 16 (1979), 81–91.

For a debate about whether God answers prayer, see the Michael Murray–
David Basinger exchange in *Contemporary Debates in Philosophy of Religion*,
eds. Michael Peterson and Raymond VanArragon (New York: Blackwell, 2003),
242–67.

Physicalism, see **materialism**.

Pluralism

Pluralism, also known as the *pluralist hypothesis*, is a response to the phenomenon of **religious diversity**. How are we to think of such diversity? How
are we to think about the competing truth claims of the different religious
traditions, to say nothing for the competing claims regarding salvation for
their adherents? Pluralism gives an answer to these questions that is both
inviting and controversial. Loosely stated, we might think of pluralism as the
thesis that all religions are different but legitimate paths to the same end.

An important defender of the pluralist hypothesis is John Hick (b. 1922).
In what follows, we will give his account of it; then we'll discuss a pair of
objections to it and conclude by briefly comparing the pluralist hypothesis to
a Buddhist approach to religious diversity.

Hick arrives at his pluralist position largely by arguing that it gives us the best
explanation of the religious diversity we see. What we see is billions of people,
across cultures and traditions, turning themselves over to an Ultimate Reality
which is the object of their honor and worship. This is a nearly universal
human tendency, one Hick takes as evidence that there really *is* such an
Ultimate Reality (the *Real*) to which people are responding, and hence that
naturalism is false. Of course, people respond in different ways and have
different beliefs about the Real, depending on the religious traditions to which
they belong. Does one particular tradition get it right, so that all the other
religions are unwittingly promoting the worship of false gods? Hick doesn't
think that this sort of **exclusivism** is the sensible position to take; indeed, he
suggests that it is morally questionable in the face of religious diversity to hold
that *your* group has it right and everyone else is mistaken, especially if you
add that only your group can attain salvation. Why would the Real favor you
and members of your group over everyone else?

Besides, Hick argues, the evidence suggests that exclusivism is false. When you back up and take an objective look at the traditions and practices of the world's main religious groups, you can see that beneath the surface they are remarkably similar and their goals are essentially the same: they aim for the transformation of their followers, from self-centeredness to "Reality-centeredness." If only one religion was genuinely in touch with the Real, we'd expect such transformation to be especially obvious among that religion's followers; but this is not what we see. Each religion has its share of sinners as well as saints. Thus we have considerable reason to deny that one religion gets it right to the exclusion of all the others.

Well then, what's the alternative? The pluralist hypothesis is that in an important sense *every* religious tradition gets it right. Each of them constitutes a legitimate response to this Ultimate Reality that they all seek. On the face of it, the different traditions make conflicting claims: Christianity sees God as a trinity, while Islam and Judaism deny this; the three theistic religions see God as a person, while Buddhism denies that the Real is personal. Since they conflict, at least some of them must be wrong. According to pluralism, strictly speaking *all* religions are mistaken in their descriptions of the Real. The problem, on Hick's view, is that this Ultimate Reality *as it is in itself* is utterly beyond us and our conceptual powers. Here Hick appeals to **Immanuel Kant's** (1724–1804) famous distinction between a thing as it is in itself and a thing as it appears to us—between what he calls the *noumena* and the *phenomena*. The Real appears to us and is accessible to us in different ways. How we perceive the Real depends largely on our upbringing and tradition, and the tradition we are a part of was itself shaped by different historical, geographical, economic, and social forces. This explains the differences between the religions. But again, the Ultimate Reality as it is in itself is utterly beyond us. Our concepts simply do not apply to it. (Note the affinity on this point with **negative theology**, the view that we can only describe God by saying what God is not.) Any religion that claims to have an accurate understanding of the Real as it is in itself is claiming to have the impossible and hence is mistaken.

To sum up, Hick's pluralist explanation of religious diversity goes like this. Near universal human religious experience provides evidence that there really is an Ultimate Reality; deep similarities among the different world religions indicate that each is in fact responding to this Reality; and differences between them, both in terms of beliefs about it and methods of response to it, provide evidence that the Real as it is in itself is beyond us, but it appears to different people differently. This explanation has profound implications for relations between religious groups: the different groups should recognize that their differences aren't essential, which should promote genuine religious dialogue and understanding.

While this response to religious diversity has its appeal, a number of objections have been raised against it. Here we'll mention two. First, the pluralist criticizes the exclusivist for saying that her religion gets it right and everyone else is wrong; but doesn't the pluralist say something quite similar? The pluralist takes a certain position about the nature of all religions and their interaction with the Real, a position that implies, among other things, that all the adherents of the great theistic religions (Christianity, Islam, Judaism) are mistaken about the God they think they're worshipping. It seems that taking *any* position on religious diversity, including the pluralist position, commits one to saying that many people's religious beliefs are false. Second, one might wonder whether the notion of an Ultimate Reality to which none of our concepts apply, which yet is such that it appears to us in different ways and is thus the source of the world's great religions—one might wonder whether such a notion makes any sense. Hick's pluralism has been rejected by some philosophers on just these grounds. Still, readers intrigued by pluralism should note that Hick has written a great deal to defend and amend his views, and that his is not the only version of the pluralist hypothesis available.

We'll conclude by comparing the pluralist position to a Buddhist approach to other religions. Pluralists discourage aggressive evangelism and emphasize the need for people to choose a religion that's right for them, since any of the world's great religions can contribute to the personal transformation that religion is really all about. Buddhists typically say something similar to this. Roughly speaking, on the Buddhist view all people are slowly progressing toward their ultimate goal, *nirvana*. It takes many lifetimes to attain this goal, which is reached through a kind of enlightenment that only Buddhists can achieve. Along the way, people may follow other religions, but the doctrines they accept can serve as *upaya*, or "skillful means," that help them move closer to the goal. Thus, even though Buddhists believe Buddhism to be superior to other religions (since only it provides the key to achieving *nirvana*), they are often content to let people stay in the religions that appeal to them, since those religions may be most appropriate to their religious development.

For a thorough explanation and defense of Hick's pluralism, see his book *A Christian Theology of Religions* (Louisville: Westminster John Knox Press, 1995). The Dalai Lama discusses a Buddhist approach to other religions in *The Bodhgaya Interviews*, Jose Ignacio Cabezon, ed. (Ithaca, NY: Snow Lion Publications, 1988).

Possible worlds

Possible worlds are simply complete descriptions of the way things could be. There are numerous ways things could be, far too many to count. Only one description of the way things could be accurately captures the way things actually are—only one such description gets it right—which is just to say that only one possible world is *actual*.

Let's spell this out a bit more. Suppose that in the actual world the Los Angeles Lakers win the NBA Championship in 2009. This is not the way that things *had* to go. Things could have been different. The Orlando Magic or Cleveland Cavaliers could have won instead. Besides, it could have taken the Lakers one fewer game than it actually took them to win. Kobe Bryant could have taken a little longer coming out of the locker room to meet with the media after the second game than he actually did. Indeed, there could have been no NBA and hence no NBA Championship. And so on. A complete description of a world that includes any of these different scenarios is a possible world. And we should emphasize that each possible world is *complete*: it doesn't merely specify whether the Lakers win in 2009, it also includes every other detail about every single thing that happens. Thus there are many possible worlds which are alike in that in them the Lakers win in 2009, but that differ on other points: in some worlds the series takes five games, while in others it takes four (or six, or seven); in some of them you exist, but in many you don't; in some there are exactly three billion pigs in the world at the moment of the opening tip-off, but in others there aren't.

Many details—infinitely many—are included in any possible world; and again only one possible world describes the way the world actually is.

The notion of possible worlds is especially important to two concepts discussed in this chapter: the **free will defense** and **Molinism**. Both of them explore the degree to which God controls which possible world is actual and the way in which giving us **libertarian freedom** limits God's creative options.

The brief account of possible worlds just given is explained in detail in **Alvin Plantinga's** *The Nature of Necessity* (New York: Oxford, 1974). A different account, where possible worlds aren't mere descriptions but real concrete things, is found in David Lewis, *On the Plurality of Worlds* (London: Blackwell, 1986). Both books are classics, but neither is for the faint of heart.

Pragmatic arguments for belief in God

Pragmatic arguments for belief in God are arguments that do not directly try to establish that God exists; instead, they try to give reasons for *believing* that God exists, whether there is good evidence for God's existence or not. Typically these pragmatic arguments claim that belief in God is somehow useful, that it is good for you to have—good either in this life or in the next. One version of the **moral argument** for belief in God concludes that you should believe in God because such belief makes you better inclined to live a moral life. **Pascal's Wager** argues that you should believe in God because of the infinite benefits that you will acquire after death if God actually exists. American philosopher **William James** (1842–1910), in his essay "**The Will to Believe**," also develops the suggestion that believing can improve your life in ways that justify your doing so.

Not all philosophers have accepted the legitimacy of pragmatic arguments. Proponents of **evidentialism** are particularly hostile, since these arguments promote belief in God in the absence of evidence, while evidentialists argue that we have a duty—perhaps even a moral one—to hold only beliefs that are based on evidence. Nonetheless, pragmatic arguments are very popular, and no doubt many religious believers, when pressed, would cite pragmatic reasons in explaining why they believe as they do.

Problem of evil

The problem of evil can be summed up as the problem that evil provides for belief in the God of **theism**. Historically, it constitutes the most profound objection to such belief, and religious believers across time and tradition have felt its force.

Before explaining the problem, we should say a few words about what we mean by "evil." In ordinary conversation when we talk about evil, we are often describing people who engage in unconscionable activities. A serial killer who gives no thought to the plight of his victims is said to be evil. The term is also used in reference to nasty supernatural phenomena in movies and the like. In philosophy of religion, however, it is helpful to think of evil simply as "bad stuff," the sort of stuff that no morally upright person would permit for its own sake. Acute pain and suffering fit this description. It may be acceptable for one who could prevent suffering to permit it if doing so is necessary to achieve some worthy end (the prevention of something worse, perhaps, or the production of some greater good), but we would question the moral character of anyone who allowed preventable suffering in the absence of such a reason. (Other phenomena may also constitute evil on this description, including bad moral character itself.) In short, while we should recognize that some evils are (much) worse than others, when thinking about the problem of evil we need to define evil rather broadly.

Philosophers also distinguish between *moral* and *natural* evil. Moral evil is evil caused by the free choices of human beings (as well as the free choices of other beings like angels or demons, if there are any). Examples include the suffering caused by a power-hungry dictator or a knife-wielding thief. Natural evil is evil caused by the workings of the natural world. Suffering caused by cancer, hurricanes, tsunamis, and the like is generally referred to as natural evil. Sometimes terrible suffering can result from the interaction of both human free will and the activities of nature, as when a person takes up smoking and later dies of lung cancer, or when a village built in a low-lying area is washed away in a flood; so the line between moral and natural evil is not a clean one.

The basic problem of evil has to do with the obvious tension between the supposed existence of a God who has the attributes of **omnipotence**,

omniscience, and **perfect goodness**, and the existence of the evil that we see. As **David Hume** (1711–76) put the problem in Book X of his *Dialogues Concerning Natural Religion*: "Is [God] willing to prevent evil, but not able? Then He is impotent. Is He able, but not willing? Then He is malevolent. Is He both able and willing? Whence then is evil?"

That gives us the basic outline of the problem of evil; but there are in fact many different ways of stating the problem and correspondingly different theistic responses to it. The **logical problem of evil** provides an argument that the mere existence of any evil at all *guarantees* that God does not exist. The **free will defense** was formulated to respond to this version of the problem by claiming that if God creates people with **libertarian freedom** (which God would have good reasons for doing), God may be unable to avoid allowing some evil to enter the world. The **evidential problem of evil** looks at the scope of evil in the world and argues that it provides solid (but not necessarily logically conclusive) evidence that God does not exist. **Theodicies** constitute attempts by theists to posit reasons God might have for permitting the evil that occurs. Finally, the so-called **existential problem of evil** has to do with the way that **horrendous evils** can drive people away from God, by motivating them to rebel against God or to reject the belief that God exists. All of these topics are covered under separate entries in this chapter. For an extended introduction to the problem of evil, see Michael L. Peterson, *God and Evil* (Boulder, CO: Westview, 1998).

Rationalism

Rationalism is a view on the relation between faith and reason that is opposed to **fideism**. While fideism asserts the primacy of faith, rationalism puts the focus on reason and emphasizes the need for faith beliefs to be supported by it.

Versions of rationalism come in degrees. A particularly strong form became popular during the Enlightenment, which took place in the Western world in the 18th century. Enlightenment thinkers, wary of the violent consequences of unchecked religious disagreement, argued that religious beliefs should conform to the new scientific worldview, which saw the world as a big machine run by deterministic physical laws. In line with this approach, many thinkers adopted deism, which claims that God exists but is not involved in the workings of the natural world. (We can see this approach taken in Thomas Jefferson's [1743–1826] *The Jefferson Bible*, where references to **miracles** and other supernatural activity in the stories about Jesus are pointedly omitted.) Others, like Baron D'Holbach (1723–89), embraced full-blooded **atheism**. D'Holbach attacked religious belief with unbridled vitriol, attacks that are echoed today in such popular books as Richard Dawkins, *The God Delusion* (New York: Houghton Mifflin, 2006) and Sam Harris, *Letter to a Christian Nation* (New York: Vintage, 2006).

More moderate versions of rationalism demand that faith beliefs be based on evidence (as required by **evidentialism**) but do not claim in advance that they must conform to an Enlightenment-style scientific worldview. Rationalists of this sort often conclude that many (if not most) faith beliefs must be abandoned since they cannot be supported by the evidence, but some believers, like **Richard Swinburne** (b. 1934), disagree and argue that the evidence actually favors the Christian faith. Other approaches to faith and reason seem to straddle the line between rationalism and fideism. **Thomas Aquinas** (1225–74), for example, viewed faith and reason as legitimate and complementary ways to truth, and held that while reason can demonstrate some religious claims (the existence of God, for example), others have to be revealed to us since reason is insufficient to establish them. (His view is set out in the first nine chapters of Book I of the **Summa Contra Gentiles**.)

Note that we have here discussed one use of the term "rationalism" in philosophy of religion; but in philosophy more generally that term usually refers to a school of thought begun by **Rene Descartes** (1596–1650) and **Gottfried Leibniz** (1646–1716) which claims that knowledge about the world can be acquired by reason employed independent of experience. Rationalism in this sense is opposed to *empiricism*, endorsed by **David Hume** (1711–76) and others, which claims that all knowledge is acquired from experience. While our kind of rationalism is related to this one, it is important to be aware that the term admits of different uses.

Reformed epistemology

The central claim of Reformed epistemology (RE) is that it is perfectly acceptable to believe in God without evidence. On this point RE rejects **evidentialism**, which claims that evidence is required for rational belief and pointedly applies that demand to religious belief, particularly belief in God. According to RE, a person can be completely justified in *starting* with belief in God, without having to argue to it. To put it another way, belief in God is innocent until proven guilty rather than, as evidentialists seem to suggest, guilty until proven innocent.

The most prominent contemporary defender of RE is **Alvin Plantinga** (b. 1932), so in what follows we'll work (in rough and ready fashion) through his arguments for it, before turning to two objections and briefly summarizing some more recent developments.

Let's first consider evidentialism. It claims that all beliefs, if they are to be justified or rational, must be based on evidence, evidence which (on the usual understanding) must take the form of *arguments*. Arguments, of course, involve premises (other beliefs) put forward in support of a conclusion. For example, according to evidentialism, to be justified or rational in believing that your ship is seaworthy you need to base that belief on evidence, perhaps the fact that the inspector said it is and the further fact that the inspector is a reliable judge of these things.

But there is a well-known problem with the evidentialist requirement: surely it can't mean that we must hold *all* our beliefs on the basis of arguments.

That would be a requirement we couldn't fulfill, since we'd need a supporting argument for every belief we hold, including for the beliefs we appeal to in those very arguments! We would support belief A with belief B, which we'd have to support with belief C, which we'd have to support with belief D, which we'd have to support . . . and on and on without end. The lesson drawn from this potentially infinite chain of beliefs is that we must be permitted to *start* with certain beliefs, beliefs that can be justified without being inferred from other beliefs. If you think of a belief system as a building, we must be allowed a foundation on which to build the rest of our beliefs. The bricks can't all rest on other bricks. Some beliefs have to be foundational, or as they are sometimes called, *basic*. We can reason from them without having to reason to them. So the question is, which beliefs require evidence, and which do not? Which beliefs can we properly start with—which beliefs are *properly* basic—and which must we reason to if we are to be justified in believing them?

To answer this question, Plantinga first turns to a prominent theory he calls *classical foundationalism*. Inspired by **Rene Descartes** (1596–1650) and others, classical foundationalism claims that the foundations of a person's belief system must be quite narrow: they can only include beliefs that we cannot be wrong about (like your belief that you exist), beliefs that are completely obvious to anyone who ponders them (like your belief that 2 + 2 = 4), or perceptual beliefs about the things around us (like your belief that you're holding a book right now). In more technical terms, classical foundationalism claims that properly basic beliefs must either be incorrigible, or self-evident, or evident to the senses. All other beliefs require evidence: they must be supported by arguments that ultimately appeal back to beliefs that are properly basic. Since belief in God clearly is not properly basic by those standards, it too must be supported by arguments; and if it is not, then it shouldn't be accepted.

So says classical foundationalism. But what if classical foundationalism is mistaken? Plantinga argues that in fact it has serious problems with it. The main problem is that it is *self-refuting* in the sense that belief in it turns out to be unjustified by its own standards. Consider the belief that classical foundationalism is true. Is that belief properly basic—that is, incorrigible, self-evident, or evident to the senses? That's doubtful. Then we need an argument in order to be justified in believing it; but it is very difficult to see what sort of argument could be offered. This problem and others, Plantinga claims, give us sufficient reason to reject classical foundationalism and return to the question that led us to it in the first place.

So, we ask again: what beliefs can we properly start with? Can we properly start with belief in God, rather than having to argue to it before we are justified in believing it? According to Plantinga, we have good reason for thinking that we can. To see this, think first about other beliefs that obviously can be properly basic, and compare those with beliefs about God. Consider, for example, perceptual beliefs about your immediate environment. You walk into a room, look around, and immediately find yourself with the belief that there are people in front of you. You don't reason or argue to that belief; instead, your visual experience simply triggers your cognitive faculties to produce that belief in you. What you do is perfectly acceptable: when you believe that way, no one objects, "Hey, you've got to have an *argument* for the belief that there are people in front of you, if you are to be justified in holding it!"

Consider also beliefs about other people. You believe very firmly that the people you interact with have minds and mental lives and feelings just like you do, but you don't come to believe that on the basis of an argument. Much work in philosophy suggests that arguments for those conclusions are much too flimsy to justify belief in them anyway; but here too it seems that arguments aren't required. Like perceptual beliefs, beliefs about other minds are automatically triggered by our experiences, and we are justified in holding them without argument. Those beliefs are properly basic, innocent until proven guilty. We are justified in believing them and reasoning from them until we have good reason for thinking that they're false.

The next step in Plantinga's argument is to suggest an **analogy**: beliefs about God are a lot like perceptual beliefs and beliefs about other people. Certain kinds of experiences can simply produce in us beliefs about God. Doing something wrong can trigger the belief that God is unhappy with you; seeing something gloriously beautiful can produce in you the belief that God is to be praised; going through certain kinds of trials can result in the belief that you need God's help. Again, these beliefs are triggered by experiences in the same way that beliefs about our physical environment or beliefs about other people's mental states are. And it seems that if *those* beliefs can rationally be held without arguments—those beliefs are innocent until proven guilty—the same should be true of beliefs about God. It would seem arbitrary and unfair to demand otherwise.

The argument so far, then, is that perceptual beliefs and beliefs about other minds are properly basic—we are justified in starting with them, and we aren't required to argue to them—and since beliefs about God are relevantly similar to those beliefs, beliefs about God can also be properly basic. But Plantinga goes further in defending this conclusion. If God exists, he argues, it would be surprising if God were to make rational theistic belief depend on a person's grasp of the complex and much-debated arguments for God's existence. One might expect God to make knowledge of God available through some other means. Following the theologian John Calvin (1509–64), Plantinga suggests that God has done just that by creating us with a *sensus divinitatus*, a "sense of the divine" that produces in us beliefs about God and grants us a natural awareness of divine activity in the world. So just as we have been created with cognitive faculties like vision and memory which produce in us beliefs about the world (and do so immediately and without depending on inferences from other beliefs), we also have a faculty that produces in us beliefs about God.

Thus, Plantinga claims, we can rationally believe in God without evidence, since such belief can be properly basic; and moreover it's sensible to suppose that such beliefs are produced by a *sensus divinitatus*, an inborn sense of the divine that is put in us by God. This position is controversial, as you can imagine; so here we'll consider two objections to it.

The first objection is to the notion that humans are naturally endowed with a *sensus divinitatus*. One would think that if this were true then there would be some agreement on God's existence and nature, and more people would find themselves with beliefs about God under similar circumstances. But of course worldwide we see enormous **religious diversity** (and many people who are not in the usual sense religious at all), and the particular religious beliefs people derive from circumstances cited above seem largely determined by their backgrounds and environments. Upon feeling guilty about something, a Christian may come to beliefs about God, while a Buddhist most likely will not. Moreover, there are plenty of people who apparently don't come to beliefs about God at all when they do something wrong, or witness beautiful scenery, or find themselves in trouble. This would be odd if we all really were endowed with a *sensus divinitatus*.

Reformed epistemologists have responded in different ways to this objection, but the main response is to point out that the *sensus divinitatus* can malfunction; there are all sorts of things that can cause it not to work well. (In this way it is just like our other cognitive faculties, such as vision, hearing, and memory.) The objection simply illustrates that for many people it does not work as well as it should. Perhaps they need divine assistance, the testimony of the church, or some kind of personal crisis to help their *sensus divinitatus* to work better or to allow them to pay better attention to what it tells them. Nonetheless, defenders of Reformed epistemology contend, the idea that God has equipped us with a natural way of knowing about God seems to fit well with the religious leanings that people in fact generally exhibit, even if the knowledge of God that it produces is weak and limited and must be supplemented by divine revelation.

A second objection to Reformed epistemology has been called the *Great Pumpkin objection*, and it goes like this. If we grant that theists can simply start with belief in God—they can be justified in believing in God without evidence—then what's to prevent someone like Linus Van Pelt from claiming the same properly basic status for his belief in the Great Pumpkin? (In case you haven't read the relevant *Peanuts* comics, Linus spends many a Halloween evening sitting in a local pumpkin patch, waiting in vain for the Great Pumpkin to come and deliver toys to the good children of the world.) In other words, Reformed epistemology effectively opens the door to the justification of any crazy belief: when pressed with the demand for evidence, believers can simply say, "My belief is innocent until proven guilty!" and perhaps even tell a story (analogous to the one about the *sensus divinitatus*) about how they came to be furnished with it.

This objection is certainly a powerful one, and it often draws people back to some form of evidentialism. What distinguishes legitimate from illegitimate religious (and other) beliefs is the evidence. Take away that requirement, and anything goes. Reformed epistemologists (Plantinga in particular) have offered responses to the Great Pumpkin objection, but rather than discuss them here we'll simply note their existence and turn finally to one more recent development in the field.

Reformed epistemology, as we have described it, makes a claim only about belief in God, arguing that such belief is properly basic. But these ideas have since been applied to other specifically Christian beliefs, including belief in the trinity and belief in particular **miracles** like the resurrection. The suggestion, developed in Plantinga's book **Warranted Christian Belief** (New York: Oxford University Press, 2000), is that those beliefs also are properly basic and can even amount to knowledge if, as Christians believe, God is responsible for producing them in us.

For more on Reformed epistemology, see Plantinga's essay, "Reason and Belief in God," found in *Faith and Rationality: Reason and Belief in God*, Alvin Plantinga and Nicholas Wolterstorff, eds. (Notre Dame, IN: University of Notre Dame Press, 1984), 16–93. For an important objection to the notion that belief in God can be properly basic for well-informed adults, see Philip Quinn, "On Finding the Foundations for Theism," *Faith and Philosophy* 2 (1985), 469–86. Michael Martin presents something like the Great Pumpkin objection in the tenth chapter of his book, *Atheism: A Philosophical Justification* (Philadelphia: Temple University Press, 1990).

Religion and science

What is the relation between religion and science? Are religion and science opposed to each other? Do they support each other? Do they have nothing to do with each other? These are important questions in philosophy of religion, because both religion and science are such powerful forces in our world, and they have historically been thought to be in tension with each other. In what follows we'll consider three positions on their relation, corresponding to the three questions just posed.

It is easy to see how religion and science might be *opposed* to each other. Advances during the Scientific Revolution were at times held up by religion, as when Galileo (1564–1642) was forced by the Church in Rome to recant his belief that the sun is at the center of the solar system. Today, the **theory of**

evolution is accepted by most scientists but emphatically rejected by the millions of Christians who endorse **creationism**, an account of the origin of the natural world which is based on a literal reading of the first chapters of the biblical book of Genesis. In addition, religious believers tend to be open to explaining events by appeal to divine intervention (and thus are open to the possible occurrence of **miracles**), while scientists are often committed to the notion that all events in the natural world can be explained in purely natural terms (they are committed, in other words, to methodological **naturalism**). Thus religious explanations appear to run counter to scientific ones.

Some people, however, think that religion and science actually *support* each other. The Scientific Revolution may be seen as an arena for conflict between religion and science, but some argue that a closer look reveals that religion actually produced the Revolution. It arose, after all, in Christian Europe in the 16th and 17th centuries, during and after the Protestant Reformation. And perhaps Christianity, with its view of a God who created the world in an orderly fashion, deserves credit for the way that scientific thinking has since developed and thrived in the West—even if at times, as poor Galileo can attest, Christians have seen conflict with science where there really isn't any. Thus it may be that religion and science are really allies deep down, despite the surface conflict.

Further, some people believe that science can help to support particular religious claims. Proponents of **intelligent design** (ID) argue that current scientific findings provide evidence that the world is the product of a designer, and hence that naturalism is false. Some creationists try to make the case that scientific study done properly supports their contention that the earth is much younger than most scientists believe. Both have made headlines in recent years, as supporters of creationism and ID have attempted without success to get their positions taught in public school science classes in the United States.

The third view claims that science and religion neither conflict with nor support each other; instead they have nothing to do with each other. One prominent proponent of this view was Stephen Jay Gould (1941–2002), a paleontologist who believed that religion and science were "non-overlapping magisteria" (NOMA). Science, he said, deals with the empirical, observable realm of the natural world, while religion deals only with questions of moral meaning and value. As such, they can't tread on each others' toes, and there is no room for conflict between them.

For more on whether science and religion conflict, see the John Worrall–Del Ratzsch exchange in *Contemporary Debates in Philosophy of Religion*, Michael Peterson and Raymond VanArragon, eds. (New York: Blackwell, 2003), 59–94. See also Stephen Jay Gould, *Rock of Ages: Science and Religion in the Fullness of Life* (New York: Ballantine Books, 2002).

Religious diversity

Religious diversity is a term whose meaning is quite obvious: it refers to the wide variety of religious traditions and followers that we see in our world today. This diversity raises significant philosophical difficulties, particularly for members of individual traditions who are trying to make sense of the others. Holding particular religious beliefs seems to commit one to saying that people who believe otherwise are mistaken; but can people with mistaken beliefs nonetheless attain salvation? And why is there such diversity, anyway? If one religion were the true one, wouldn't its superiority be more obvious? These questions are especially pressing in our day, since believers often live side by side with members of other religious groups and, in many cases, are able to see the vibrancy of their religious lives in ways that previous generations could not. There are a number of positions available on the issue of the legitimacy of other religions, including **exclusivism**, which holds one's own religion as the unique source of truth and the only avenue to salvation; **inclusivism**, which holds to the unique truth of one's own religion but acknowledges that members of other religious groups can achieve salvation; and **pluralism**, which holds that all the major religious traditions are essentially different roads to the same end.

Religious experience

Religious experience is the sort of experience people have that leads them to think that they have been in contact with the divine. Such experiences can be relatively mundane, as when a person experiences a feeling of comfort that he attributes to the work of God, or quite dramatic, as when a person has an ecstatic vision that she believes gives her some profound insight into the divine. Such experiences are often essential to the religious faith of those who have them. Philosophical issues arise about them, however, when we ponder how to determine their legitimacy. Do they provide evidence for the existence of God or some other divine reality? Are they reliable sources of religious truth? How can they be checked?

There are at least two potential problems for the suggestion that religious experiences really get us in touch with the divine. The first is the possibility of natural explanations of such experiences. Advances in scientific understanding have led many people to be suspicious of supposed divine intervention in the natural world (and hence to be suspicious of **miracle** stories); and perhaps the same suspicions should be applied here. A person who under great stress feels a wave of comfort may just be experiencing a natural reaction generated in his brain as a sort of coping mechanism to help him get through trouble. Dramatic visions may have a similar source, or may on the other hand be due to drug use or some kind of illness.

A second problem, connected to the first, is that the incredible variety of religious experiences lends credence to natural explanations of them. If those experiences were caused by a single divine reality, we'd expect more uniformity than we see. Michael Martin (b. 1932) points out that even though drug users sometimes say that the drugs put them in touch with a divine reality, that claim is called into question by the lack of uniformity in such experiences and by our inability to provide a coherent story of how and why a divine reality would produce such a variety of experiences under such strange circumstances. The same goes, he argues, for religious experiences. The differences between them and the difficulty of explaining how they may be produced by a single divine reality should lead us to think that their source is simply the individual minds of those who have them.

Still, religious experiences can be extraordinarily convicting and life- changing. Couldn't they put their subjects in touch with the divine even if they do at the same time admit of natural explanations? And can't we have reason for thinking that some are in this way legitimate even if, clearly, not all of them are? For further reading on kinds of religious experience and their effects, see **William James'** classic, *The Varieties of Religious Experience* (Scott's Valley,

CA: IAP, 2009 [1902]) and the autobiography of **Teresa of Avila**, *The Life of St. Teresa of Avila*, J. M. Cohen, trans. (New York: Penguin, 1957). For an argument from religious experience for belief in God, see the thirteenth chapter of **Richard Swinburne's *The Existence of God*** 2nd ed. (New York: Oxford University Press, 2004). Michael Martin offers a critique of that argument in his book *Atheism: A Philosophical Justification* (Philadelphia: Temple University Press, 1990).

Substance dualism, see **dualism**.

Teleological argument

The teleological argument, also known as the argument from design, is one of the great arguments for God's existence. In fact, the teleological argument is a family of arguments, each of which points to some feature of the physical world and argues that it appears to exhibit design, purpose, or function (*telos*), and hence provides evidence for a supernatural designer. (The **intelligent design** (ID) movement can be seen in part as promoting different versions of the teleological argument.) Here we'll look at two basic versions of the teleological argument and some criticisms of them.

The first kind of argument focuses on particular creatures (and their parts) and argues that they must have been designed. A famous version of this argument comes courtesy of **William Paley** (1743–1805), a British philosopher who argued that just as study of a watch should yield the conclusion that it is the product of design, so should study of animals yield the conclusion that they are the products of design. In other words, Paley gives us an **analogy**: he points out that animals are like watches in the way that their parts work together in the service of obvious functions (in the case of an animal, to enable it to live and reproduce; in the case of the watch, to enable it to keep and display the time). If they are alike in this way, we should conclude that they are alike in being the products of design as well. Moreover, given the variety and complexity of living creatures, their designer must be quite impressive—something like God.

This version of the argument is met head-on by the **theory of evolution**, which offers a purely natural explanation of how living things developed the features that they have. In short, it claims that these creatures were designed by an impersonal process that weeded out maladaptive creatures and characteristics, and allowed appropriately functioning creatures to carry on and reproduce. Thus critics of this version of the teleological argument claim that the theory of evolution removes any need to explain the characteristics of living things by appealing to the activity of a divine being.

This response has not ended the debate. Proponents of intelligent design have attempted to revive the argument by claiming that certain biological systems utilized in nature cannot have been produced by evolutionary processes, and must have required the intervention of a supernatural agent. (The entry on intelligent design goes into more detail on how they attempt to do this.) Others have pointed to the mind-boggling complexity of the basic building-blocks of living things, like cells, and argued that it is highly unlikely that they should come to be by chance, through the activity of purely natural forces. Hence the first kind of teleological argument continues to be hotly debated.

A second version of the teleological argument appeals to more global features of our universe. The great philosopher and skeptic **David Hume** (1711–76), in *Dialogues Concerning Natural Religion*, has one of his characters elegantly propose that the universe is like a machine and as such must have a designer. After questioning the analogy (do we have enough knowledge of the universe to reliably compare it to a machine?), other characters contend that even if the argument were successful, it would not prove the existence of God. After all, the designer of the universe, if it's like designers of earthly machines, must have a body; there may be a committee rather than a single designer; this universe with all its apparent flaws may have been created by an infant god taking his first crack at world-making rather than the God of **theism**. Answers to Hume's objections have been proposed, but what he says does indicate that the teleological argument must be supplemented in order to establish that the designer in question is God.

In recent years, the teleological argument based on large-scale features of the universe has gone well beyond Hume's presentation of it. The so-called *fine-tuning argument* points in particular to the fact that the physical laws that operate in our universe—the forces working at the time of the Big Bang, the event that many scientists believe started the universe over twelve billion years ago—had to be almost exactly as they were in order for the universe to develop and be hospitable to life as we know it. To understand the incredible degree of fine-tuning involved, it's helpful to imagine, say, fifty large dials on a wall, all of which are set differently and must be set within a millimeter of where they are in order for the universe to be suitable for life. If any of them are off in the slightest way from these narrow parameters, then the Big Bang will not explode as necessary, and the resulting universe will instead simply collapse in on itself or else explode outward with such force that it is impossible for bodies (like stars and planets) to form. In either case, it will be impossible for life to exist. So, the fine-tuning teleological argument points out, as a matter of fact the dials were set *exactly* right, exactly so that a universe capable of producing and sustaining life would be generated. (Not only that: the universe actually *produced* life! It's one thing for a universe to be capable of producing life; it's another thing for the universe actually to produce it.) What should we make of this?

The sensible thing to conclude, according to the argument, is that the dials were intentionally set by someone—or, to step away from our helpful picture a moment, that the physical forces guiding the development of our universe were the product of design. It would be monumentally improbable for the forces to be set that way by accident; and so we should conclude that it was a set-up. It was designed, which means there is a cosmic designer, God.

The fine-tuning argument is one of the most powerful versions of the teleological argument, and these days it is widely discussed. But it is not without its critics. A significant objection suggests that in fact there are (either now or spread out through time) many universes and big bangs—perhaps infinitely many—and if so it wouldn't be terribly surprising if some of them, by pure chance, should turn out to be conducive to life. If you roll a handful of dice over and over again, it is not surprising when eventually, by chance, they turn up all sixes! Maybe so, defenders of the argument respond; but what reason do we have for thinking that there *are* many universes? Without further evidence, we should assume that there is one universe, and, as the argument shows, that it is the product of design.

For further defense of the fine-tuning argument, see Robin Collins, "The Fine-tuning Design Argument" in *Reason for the Hope Within*, Michael J. Murray, ed. (Grand Rapids, MI: Eerdmans, 1999). For a critique, see chapters 8 and 9 of Peter van Inwagen's *Metaphysics* 3rd ed. (Boulder, CO: Westview, 2008).

Theism

Theism is the belief that God exists, where God is the greatest possible being, the epitome of perfection, the immaterial creator of everything other than God, a being whose essential attributes include **omnipotence**, **omniscience**, and **perfect goodness**. (This view of God is often called *classical theism*, although that label sometimes refers more narrowly to the medieval view discussed in the next paragraph. The belief that theism is false is known as **atheism**, while **agnosticism** is the stance taken by those who withhold belief on whether God exists or not.) Theism is held in common by three great religions, Christianity, Judaism, and Islam, though they differ on some specific characteristics of God (whether God is a trinity, for example) and the nature of God's revelation to humanity. Much work in philosophy of religion has been dedicated to exploring theism, its meaning, its coherence (that is, whether it makes sense), and the rationality of accepting it.

Proponents of theism all agree that God is the greatest possible being, but views on what that means have shifted somewhat over the years. We can see this when we consider the ways that some contemporary theists disagree with medieval theists on what attributes a perfect God must have. On the nature of **God and time**, notable medieval theologians without exception believed God to be outside time, while contemporary thinkers are more open to the possibility that God is in time like we are. (Many agree with the medieval view, but some do not.) Medieval scholars also believed God has the attributes of immutability (changelessness) and impassivity (lack of emotion), while contemporary thinkers regularly reject them both. In addition, while earlier theists were unanimous in understanding omniscience to include comprehensive knowledge of the future, **open theism**, which claims God is omniscient but lacking foreknowledge, is becoming quite popular today. Thus debate continues among theists on how to characterize the divine attributes.

For a classic exploration and defense of theism, see **Richard Swinburne**, *The Coherence of Theism* rev. ed. (New York: Oxford University Press, 1993).

Theodicies

Theodicies are explanations of why God allows evil—they "justify the ways of God" to humans. They thus constitute responses to the **problem of evil**. Evil and suffering are obvious features of our world that seem to be in tension with the existence of an **omnipotent**, **omniscient**, **perfectly good** God. But if theists can come up with a good reason God might have for permitting the evil that we see—both natural evil and moral evil—that would help solve the problem and render the existence of said evil ineffective as evidence against God's existence. (Not only that: there would also be value, for theists, in understanding to some degree the mysterious ways of God.)

Numerous theodicies have been proposed over the centuries, and here we shall just discuss two of them. Both are rooted in the Christian tradition. The first is an *Augustinian* theodicy, named after **St. Augustine** (354–430) whose influential version remains standard among many Christians today. The second is an *Irenaean* theodicy, named after Irenaeus (2nd century, dates uncertain), whose views on the subject were eclipsed by Augustine's but have received new life in recent decades. Variations on both theodicies are possible and available, but here it is appropriate simply to highlight elements of these basic options.

The Augustinian theodicy sees human sin as the original cause of evil on earth. God created the world perfect, as a glorious habitat for human beings (and God) to enjoy; thus God did not *create* evil. (Evil is not a *thing*, anyway; it's merely the absence of good. Similarly, darkness is not a thing, but is the absence of light.) But God also gave people **free will** to either worship God or to turn away in sinful disobedience and pride, to either use God's creation for good or to twist it and use it for ill. They chose the latter, in a catastrophic event known as the Fall. The Fall brought evil into the world: nature became harsh toward itself and toward us (thus natural evil is ultimately moral evil, caused by free human choices), and the descendents of the first humans were born with original sin, which rendered them both corrupt and guilty (and thus deserving of eternal **hell**). Fortunately, God enacted a plan to redeem the world and return it to its original state. That plan involved the incarnation, where God became human in the person of Jesus Christ, and it will eventually include the separation of those people who will be damned to hell from those who will be granted salvation and spend eternity in the glorious surroundings of heaven.

The key points then: God did not create evil; evil entered the originally perfect world by virtue of human sin (a misuse of free will); and God will recreate that perfect world in heaven, where the blessed will spend eternity after death. But while this accounts for the origin of evil, how it entered the world, it doesn't yet explain why God allowed all this to happen in the first place. What's the explanation for that? In answer to this question, a number of themes show up in Augustine's writing and in the writings of followers who have endorsed his style of theodicy. First, with free will comes the possibility of evil, a risk God was willing to take given the enormous value of free will. (This point is not easy to reconcile with a strong view of **divine providence** or with a **compatibilist** account of human freedom, which some proponents of this theodicy seem to accept. After all, if compatibilism is true, then people can have free will and at the same time God can cause them to do exactly what God wants them to do.) Second, the overall picture, with some people justly ending up in hell for their sins while some others are mercifully saved, enables God to demonstrate God's greatness by exhibiting the twin virtues of justice and mercy. Third—and here the limits of human understanding come clearly into play—the overall picture, with its good and bad parts, its light and dark shades, looks beautiful to God, even if we cannot see it ourselves.

That, in brief, is the Augustinian theodicy, a highly influential picture despite the mystery inherent in it and the questions that can be raised both about the role free will plays in it and about the portrayal of God it sets forth.

The second theodicy is an Irenaean theodicy, developed in recent years by **John Hick** (b. 1922). Interestingly, a principle reason Hick gives for rejecting the Augustinian picture is that our current scientific understanding of the history of our planet indicates that at no time in the past was the world "perfect," and moreover it is clear that there was suffering and bloodshed in nature long before any humans showed up and had the chance to fall. In light of this, Hick's Irenaean theodicy does not posit that the created world was originally perfect; instead, it claims that the world has always been a harsh environment and the human beings placed in it were created flawed and immature, but with enormous potential for moral and spiritual development. Promoting this development is in fact the whole point of evil. The goal God has for human beings is that they develop moral virtue and genuine religious faith; and this sort of growth is only possible in a challenging environment. To put it another way, God allows evil for the sake of *soul-making*; without evil, God would be unable to produce the kind of people God wants.

We can see the plausibility of Hick's suggestion when we consider what is required for raising character-filled children. Giving children everything they want, not requiring effort from them, and allowing them to live in a "paradise" tends to turn them into spoiled brats. Nobody wants that! To avoid this, parents are advised to give their children chores, to allow them choices, to let them deal with the consequences—because such hardships help develop children into responsible citizens who see a world outside of their own needs and desires.

The Irenaean theodicy suggests, in effect, that this is what God has done with us. God has placed us in a world that runs in accord with physical laws which create hardships for us while at the same time providing us with resources to deal with them. God has also given us free will, so that we might choose for ourselves how we are going to deal with nature and with each other. And, in an understandable twist, God has placed a certain "epistemic distance" between us and God, so that God's existence and intentions are not entirely clear to us. Doing this opens the way again for us to make our own choices, either to turn in faith to God or to care only for ourselves and our present circumstances.

That, in brief, is the theodicy Hick presents to us. A number of questions can be raised about it. First, if soul-making is the reason God allows evil, why is there *so much* evil? To return to our child-rearing analogy, there are limits to how much we subject children to in order to build their character. Giving children chores seems acceptable, but the suffering human beings endure goes far beyond that! Second, and related, what shall we make of evils that don't make souls but instead destroy them? (**Horrendous evils**, as described by **Marilyn McCord Adams** (b. 1943) fit this mold: they are too awful to contribute to soul-making.) Suppose a person experiences some horror and as a result, rather than turning toward God she turns away and dies in grief and misery. What reason could God have for allowing *that* evil? Hick's response to this question, interestingly enough, is to invoke **universalism**: the soul-making process may not be completed in this life, but God will continue to work on people afterwards (and presumably use evil in the process) until they eventually become what God desires for them to be.

Many other theodicies have been offered, and readers are invited to ponder them and their prospects for success. A pair of interesting examples are **C. S. Lewis**, *The Problem of Pain* (New York: HarperOne, 2001 [1940]) and Peter van Inwagen, "The Magnitude, Duration, and Distribution of Evil," in his book *God, Knowledge, and Mystery* (Ithaca, NY: Cornell, 1995).

Theory of evolution

The theory of evolution is the scientific theory that explains the progressive development of life on earth. Formulated and inspired by Charles Darwin (1809–82), the theory has been enormously important in the natural sciences, but also in philosophy of religion. Here we'll look at two ways in which this has been so.

The first is that the theory of evolution provides **atheists** and others a response to a powerful version of the **teleological argument**. The argument states, in essence, that apparent design of living things—the ways that they are particularly suited to their environments, seemingly engineered to survive and reproduce—provides good evidence that they were designed and hence that there is a designer (God). The theory of evolution explains how these creatures could appear to be designed when in fact they aren't—not by any supernatural agent, anyway. The explanation goes something like this. Suppose you start with one species of animal. Its environment is always changing, so that there are different sources of food and different predators hunting it. But the species changes, too. Offspring may be born with features that its parents didn't have, as the result of what are called *random genetic mutations*. Some of these new features may help the animals to survive and reproduce (possibly passing on those characteristics to their own offspring), and others may not. So, for example, if an animal is born with exceptionally large feet (or the propensity to develop them), that might make it a really slow runner, easily killed by predators, in which case it likely won't survive and pass on that trait. On the other hand, if it is born with larger fangs, that might make predators less likely to attack it, which would be a happy result for it and its descendents. The key point here is that *nature* determines which traits, and which creatures that have them, survive. Hence the notion of *natural selection*, which gives us a perfect explanation of how animals seem so well adapted to their environments. Nature selects those creatures with suitable characteristics, and the rest die off. Nothing supernatural is involved. And so, critics of the teleological argument say, that argument has been answered: we can explain the remarkable features of the creatures we see without making any appeal to God.

So, clearly, the theory of evolution is relevant to the philosophy of religion in the way that it provides non-theists a scientific explanation of the development of life on earth. This does not mean, however, that endorsing **theism** commits one to rejecting the theory. On this point we encounter a second way in which the theory is relevant: it raises important questions about the compatibility of faith and reason, and particularly of **religion and science**. Theists have differed among themselves over how much of the theory, if any, they are able to accept. **Creationists**—Christians who accept a literal reading of the biblical book of Genesis—chafe at the theory because it implies that life took a long, long, time to develop into its current forms, much longer than their own view allows for. Other Christians worry that the evolutionary story, which implies that creatures were suffering and dying long before humans showed up on the scene, makes trouble for traditional Augustinian **theodicies** (explanations of why God allows evil). Still other theists are concerned that the theory leaves no room for divine activity—and indeed some prominent advocates of the theory argue that it rules out God entirely. Opposing them, proponents of **intelligent design** argue that scientific evidence indicates that a designer must have intervened at certain points in the history of life, and hence that the theory cannot in fact give a comprehensive naturalistic explanation of life as we know it.

Thus debates over evolution and its implications for religion rage on, in the public square (particularly in the United States) and in academic discussions as well. For a classic defense of the theory of evolution, see Richard Dawkins' book, *The Blind Watchmaker: Why the Evidence of Evolution Reveals a Universe without Design* (New York: Norton, 1996). For an atheist's exploration of some of the theory's implications, see Daniel Dennett, *Darwin's Dangerous Idea* (New York: Touchstone, 1995).

Universalism

Universalism, a minority though perhaps increasingly popular view among Christians, states that there is no eternal **hell** and that all people will eventually attain salvation. Here we shall consider two arguments for universalism.

The first argument claims that no one could possibly deserve to suffer eternally in hell, and hence it would be entirely unjust for God to allow anyone to do so. Think about it: to punish convicted murderers we send them to prison for a few decades. That is steep punishment, but many of us think it fair since murder is one of the worst crimes a person can commit. But that punishment is nothing at all compared with hell. A few decades aren't even a drop in the bucket of eternity! How can anyone do anything so terrible as to merit punishment that literally never ends? Such punishment would be patently unjust, the argument goes, and hence God would not allow it.

The second argument focuses less on justice and more on God's love and power. As a loving creator, God desires the salvation of all persons. God is able to achieve the salvation of all persons, and hence God will do so. Of course, saving a particular person may require that person's free cooperation, and it seems that many people on earth die while in a state of rebellion toward God. But God is not confined to working within the framework of earthly lives; nothing prevents God from pursuing people and soliciting their acceptance of salvation after their deaths. Given enough time, surely God's intentions will be fulfilled.

For an important recent defense of universalism, see **Marilyn McCord Adams**, "The Problem of Hell: A Problem of Evil for Christians," in *Reasoned Faith*, Eleonore Stump, ed. (Ithaca, NY: Cornell University Press, 1993). There Adams argues that a loving God would ensure that every created person's life would be worth living, from the perspective of that person. A person who spends eternity in hell would not enjoy such a life. See also *Universal Salvation: The Current Debate*, Robin A. Parry and Christopher H. Partridge, eds. (Grand Rapids: Eerdmans, 2004), where Thomas Talbott defends universalism from objections presented by a number of philosophers and theologians.

Key Thinkers in Philosophy of Religion

This chapter highlights a number of important philosophers and theologians, and shows how they connect with terms and concepts discussed in the previous chapter.

Adams, Marilyn McCord (b. 1943)

Marilyn McCord is a prominent contemporary philosopher who has spent most of her career teaching at UCLA, Yale University, and Oxford University. In philosophy of religion she has made especially important contributions to discussions of the **problem of evil** and **hell**. With the problem of evil, she has argued that many **theodicies** focus too much attention on global goods—like making the world a better place—that God can acquire by allowing evil, and ignore the individuals whose lives seem to be destroyed by it. Hence much of her work has been dedicated to responding to the problem of **horrendous evils**, evils which call into question whether the lives of those who experience them can be good for them over all. Her concern about hell has followed from this, since hell seems a splendid example of a horrendous evil: How can a person's life (that is, his entire existence) be good for him if he ends up spending eternity in hell? Adams claims that such a life can't be a good for a person who lives it, and she argues that a perfectly good and loving God would not let a person endure such a life. In this way, she defends **universalism**, which denies the existence of an eternal hell. Her book *Horrendous Evils and the Goodness of God* (Ithaca: Cornell University Press, 2000) contains material on both of these positions.

Adams, Robert M. (b. 1937)

Robert M. Adams is a philosopher who has made important contributions in many areas of philosophy of religion. He has taught at the University of

Michigan as well as UCLA and Yale. He is well-known in philosophical circles for developing a sophisticated version of the **moral argument** for belief in God, for defending **divine command theory** in religious ethics, for pushing the "grounding objection" against **Molinism**, and for many other things besides. Important essays of his are often found in philosophy of religion anthologies, and are collected in his book, *The Virtue of Faith and Other Essays in Philosophical Theology* (New York: Oxford University Press, 1987).

Anselm (1033–1109)

St. Anselm, Archbishop of Canterbury, was one of the most important philosophical theologians of the Middle Ages. He did much reflection on the relation of faith and reason; he endorsed the position of "faith seeking understanding" (also held by **Augustine** [354–430]), where faith is seen as primary and reason serves faith by helping one to comprehend its deliverances. Hence with the extremes on the relation of faith and reason being **fideism** and **rationalism**, Anselm leaned toward the former but thought that reason could help us to understand what God reveals to be true. Anselm applied this perspective to his own faith beliefs: he sought to explain the atonement (the way in which, as Christians believe, Christ's death and resurrection atoned for human sin) in *Cur Deus Homo* (Why God became Human); and in *Proslogium* he applied reason to his belief in God by developing the famous **ontological argument**.

Aquinas, Thomas (1225–74)

A great medieval philosopher and a genius of the first order, St. Thomas Aquinas was a Dominican monk who taught at the University of Paris. In his day, the works of **Aristotle** (384–322 B.C.E.) had been recovered in the West; for centuries they had been studied by Islamic philosophers but had been passed to Western Europeans as a result of interactions between the two civilizations. While many theologians believed that Christian faith and Aristotelian philosophy could not be reconciled, Aquinas thought that they could, and a good deal of his work was dedicated to synthesizing the two.

Aquinas is famous for numerous contributions to philosophy of religion. On faith and reason, he held a stronger view of reason than some of his predecessors in so far as he thought that reason could by itself demonstrate some of the claims of Christian faith. Reason could establish God's existence, for example, and could also, unaided by revelation, discover the **natural law** which dictates how things in the natural world, especially us, need to act in order to flourish. Faith, given to us by way of divine revelation, was still needed to arrive at important Christian claims like the trinity and the resurrection. Still, faith and reason were complementary ways of getting to the truth and, on Aquinas's view, they could not conflict.

Aquinas also had important things to say on nearly every significant issue in philosophy of religion, and his way of looking at the world remains hugely influential, especially in the theology of the Roman Catholic Church. Readers are recommended to consult any of the philosophy of religion anthologies mentioned in the first chapter to find some introductory readings from Aquinas. See also the entry in the next chapter on his great volumes, the *Summa Contra Gentiles* and the *Summa Theologica*.

Aristotle (384–322 B.C.E.)

Aristotle was one of the three giants of Greek philosophy, following Socrates (469–399 B.C.E.) and **Plato** (427–347 B.C.E). Though he was Plato's student he differed from Plato on crucial points, including on issues in **metaphysics** where Plato emphasized the non-material and Aristotle emphasized the material realm of reality. (This difference is captured in the great painting, *School of Athens*, by Raphael (1483–1520), where Plato and Aristotle are pictured together, with Plato pointing to the heavens and Aristotle gesturing toward the earth.) In philosophy of religion, Aristotle serves as an important background to **Aquinas** (1225–74); like Aquinas, he gave a version of the **cosmological argument** (Aristotle did not think the world had a beginning, though he did think it is dependent on a First Cause), and he also presented an ethical theory which sees the purpose of human life to be central to understanding the nature of moral virtue and moral behavior. Aristotle's extant writings are actually lecture notes and hence not especially accessible; but *Nichomachean Ethics* is one exception that contains his fascinating discussion of happiness, human function, and virtue. For an excellent comprehensive explanation of Aristotle's philosophy, see Jonathan Lear, *Aristotle: The Desire to Understand* (New York: Cambridge University Press, 1988).

Augustine (354–430)

St. Augustine of Hippo was probably the most important philosophical theologian of his time, and his pronouncements on many issues became the
standard positions of the Christian church in the Western world. Born in
northern Africa, he converted to Christianity as a young man, served for years
as a bishop in the church, and died during the time when the Roman Empire
was being overrun by barbarian tribes from northern Europe. Prior to his conversion, he endorsed Manichaeism, a version of cosmic **dualism** which held
the world to be controlled by equal but opposed good and evil forces. His
later acceptance of Platonism paved the way for his conversion (as he details
in his *Confessions*) by helping him begin to make sense of the **problem of
evil**. Augustine's **theodicy**—his explanation of why God allows evil—remains
popular among Western Christians today, particularly his view that the world
was created perfect, that evil entered it as a result of human sin, and that
human beings ever after suffered from the effects of original sin. In addition,
Calvinists, with their strong view of **divine providence** and relatively weak
view of human **free will**, often cite Augustine as an inspiration. Aside from
Confessions, readers interested in Augustine's take on free will might try *On
Free Choice of the Will*, Thomas Williams, trans. (Indianapolis: Hacket, 1993).

Avicenna (981–1037)

Avicenna was one of a number of great Islamic philosophers who applied the
work of **Aristotle** (384–322 B.C.E.) to Islamic thought and had considerable
impact on philosophy in the Christian West as a result. (Later Christians
learned much about Aristotle by reading work of the Islamic philosophers.)
He spent much of his life in or near present-day Iran, and was a renowned
scholar and authority in fields of study from mathematics to medicine. In
philosophy of religion, he proposed early versions of the **ontological** and
cosmological arguments (one similar to the version attributed to Leibniz
in the previous chapter) for God's existence, and also offered an argument
for substance **dualism** that anticipated one put forward centuries later by
Rene Descartes (1596–1650). For more on Avicenna, see the *Cambridge
Companion to Arabic Philosophy*, Peter Adamson and Richard Taylor, eds.
(Cambridge: Cambridge University Press, 2005), a book which includes a
stellar introduction to all the great Islamic philosophers and the issues that
concerned them.

Clifford, W. K. (1845–79)

W. K. Clifford, a British mathematician and philosopher, is well-known in philosophy of religion mainly for his emphatic adherence to **evidentialism**, expressed in his assertion that "it is always wrong, everywhere and for anyone, to believe anything on insufficient evidence." Clifford's arguments have challenged religious philosophers since then either to present sufficient evidence that their religious beliefs are true, or to show that it is not in fact wrong to believe without such evidence. His views were explicitly criticized by **William James** (1842–1910) in **"The Will to Believe**." Clifford's "The Ethics of Belief" is in the public domain and is reprinted in numerous philosophy of religion anthologies.

Craig, William Lane (b. 1949)

William Lane Craig is an important contemporary Christian apologist who has done much to defend Christian claims in writing and in public debate. Much of his work has focused on arguments for God's existence, and he earned fame in philosophical circles for reviving and developing the *kalam* **cosmological argument**. He has also defended more specific Christian beliefs, including belief in the **miraculous** resurrection of Jesus. In addition, he has contributed to many discussions among Christian philosophers, defending **Molinism** in the debate over the nature of **divine providence**, and arguing, with respect to **God and time**, that God is eternal without the creation but since creation is in time and affected by it. Craig is the author of many books, including *Reasonable Faith: Christian Truth and Apologetics* 3rd ed. (Wheaton, IL: Crossway Books, 2008), which is an accessible defense of Christian belief. See also Craig's debate with Walter Sinnott-Armstrong in *God?: A Debate between a Christian and an Atheist* (New York: Oxford, 2004).

Descartes, René (1596–1650)

René Descartes was a brilliant French philosopher and mathematician, often called the father of modern philosophy. For some, this is not a compliment, since modern philosophy tends toward **evidentialism** and skepticism, and in general sets reason over faith. Descartes is well-known even outside of academic circles for making the curious statement, "I think, therefore I am." This statement is actually extremely important, since it established for Descartes the absolute foundation of his beliefs, the belief about which he could not be mistaken. Descartes also developed a version of the **ontological argument** and gave a spirited defense of substance **dualism**, both of which can be found in his ***Meditations on First Philosophy***.

Freud, Sigmund (1856–1939)

The father of modern psychoanalysis, Freud is famous for his theories about the hidden factors that motivate human belief and behavior. In philosophy of religion, he cast a suspicious eye toward religious belief, and argued that it was produced by wish-fulfillment. Human beings are very needy: life is difficult and tenuous; people fail us; nature is threatening; and bad people seem to prosper. In response to these needs, we essentially create gods who offer protection and who can set things right in the afterlife. Freud believed that this response to the human predicament is perfectly natural but that religion itself is an illusion, and that we should recognize that it is. He presented this influential account of religious belief in *The Future of an Illusion* (New York: Classic Books, 2009 [1927]).

Hick, John (b. 1922)

John Hick, for many years a professor at Claremont Graduate School in California, is a controversial and important thinker on the **problem of evil** and especially the issue of **religious diversity**. His notable achievements include breathing new life into the Irenaean **theodicy** and developing and defending a highly influential version of **pluralism** (or the pluralist hypothesis) according to which all major religions are legitimate responses to the same ultimate religious reality. His books include *Evil and the God of Love* rev. ed. (New York: Palgrave MacMillan, 2007), and *A Christian Theology of Religions* (Louisville: Westminster John Knox Press, 1995).

Hume, David (1711–76)

Scottish philosopher David Hume's influence on contemporary philosophy is difficult to overstate. He was one of the great empiricists of the modern period, which means that he believed that whatever knowledge we have is acquired from experience. He also was a skeptic: he believed that we don't know, and aren't justified in believing, much at all. This skepticism spread to religion. He is famous for providing a powerful critique of the **teleological argument**, for his statement of the **problem of evil**, and for his objections to belief in **miracles**. Many of his most important writings on these topics can be found in his ***Dialogues Concerning Natural Religion***, though his essay "Of Miracles" is found in *An Enquiry Concerning Human Understanding*.

James, William (1842–1910)

William James was an American philosopher who endorsed a view known as pragmatism. Roughly speaking, this means that he was interested in evaluating philosophical claims by looking at their practical consequences. This approach is adopted in **pragmatic arguments for belief in God**, which appeal to the benefits of such belief as reason to adopt it, rather than providing evidence that God in fact exists. James himself, in his essay "**The Will to Believe**" provided such an argument. He is also well-known in philosophy of religion for his book *The Varieties of Religious Experience* (Scott's Valley, CA: IAP, 2009 [1902]) which explores some of the effects of religious belief on the feelings and experiences of believers.

Kant, Immanuel (1724–1804)

Immanuel Kant was one of the greatest and most influential philosophers of the last 300 years. A German Christian, he made important contributions in nearly all areas of philosophy. In the fields of **epistemology** and **metaphysics** he argued that the way we experience the world is dictated not by the world itself but by the structures of our own minds. As a result of the workings of our minds, things appear to us as if they are located in space and time; but we must recognize that those are mere appearances and not the way the things really are in themselves. Kant drew the distinction, then, between the *phenomena* and the *noumena*, between things as they appear to us and things as they are in themselves. The former we can study, but the latter is closed off to us. This distinction is used in philosophy of religion in **John Hick's** (b. 1922) discussion of **pluralism**: we can know, Hick says, how the Ultimate Reality appears to different religious groups, but we cannot know what it is like in itself.

Kant is also important to the philosophy of religion because of his objections to the major arguments for God's existence: the **cosmological**, **teleological**, and especially the **ontological arguments**. With the last, he is famous for claiming that the ontological argument depends on the mistaken supposition that "existence" is a predicate or property that can be added to a thing. His rejections of these arguments reflect his views about the limits of human reason. Despite this, he proposed a **moral argument** for belief in God and human **immortality**. Roughly speaking, in order to make sense of the moral law, we need to postulate the existence of a God who will ensure in the next life that virtue is rewarded with happiness.

Kant's own writings are prohibitively difficult for beginners (and for experts as well!), but those interested in exploring his ideas further are encouraged to check out Roger Scruton, *Kant: A Very Short Introduction* (New York: Oxford University Press, 2001).

Kierkegaard, Søren (1813–55)

Søren Kierkegaard was a Danish philosopher whose ideas became very influential in the 20th century, well after his death. He is known as one of the precursors of *existentialism*, a school of thought that emphasizes our need to create ourselves through our own choices. (Famous existentialists of the 20th century include Jean-Paul Sartre [1905–80] and Albert Camus [1913–60].) Kierkegaard was also a **fideist** who believed that Christian faith requires a "leap" that goes beyond what reason can justify or comprehend. The central claims of Christianity—in particular the notion that God, an eternal, infinite being became human, temporal, and finite—are paradoxical and even offensive to reason. Because of this, faith that those claims are true must be given to us by God, though continually accepting and living by faith is a choice that is up to us. One of Kierkegaard's best-known works is *Fear and Trembling*, C. Stephen Evans and Sylvia Walsh, eds. (New York: Cambridge, 2006). For a helpful guide to Kierkegaard's thinking, see C. Stephen Evans, *Kierkegaard: An Introduction* (Cambridge: Cambridge University Press, 2009).

Leibniz, Gottfried (1646–1716)

Leibniz was a German philosopher and mathematician best known for invent-
ing calculus. In philosophy, he followed **Rene Descartes** (1596–1650) in
endorsing a kind of **rationalism** that holds that we can acquire knowledge
of the world independent of experience. In philosophy of religion he developed a version of the **cosmological argument** that depends on a principle
of sufficient reason which states, roughly, that all positive facts must have an
explanation. (This principle actually plays a central role in Leibniz's entire philosophy.) Leibniz also came up with a **theodicy** in response to the **problem
of evil**. For him the puzzle was how God, who must create the best **possible
world**, could end up creating this one. Leibniz contended that this world
actually *is* the best possible world. In response to those who claim that it isn't,
Leibniz argued that they do not know enough about how the world as a
whole would be different if certain terrible events didn't happen in it, and
hence cannot make the case the God could have created a better world than
this one. His arguments can be found in his book *Theodicy*, E. M. Huggard,
trans. (Chicago: Open Court, 1998), excerpts from which are often found in
philosophy of religion anthologies.

Lewis, C. S. (1898–1963)

C. S. Lewis, a British scholar and author of the Narnia series of children's
books, was one of the most popular Christian writers of his day and remains
popular even now. He was especially gifted at stating complex philosophical
arguments in ordinary but elegant language. In philosophy of religion, he is
best known for presenting a version of the **moral argument** for God's existence, for defending belief in **miracles**, and for developing an argument
against **naturalism** that is quite similar to the recent and widely discussed
evolutionary argument against naturalism. (For an accessible introduction to Lewis's argument, see Victor Reppert, *C.S. Lewis's Dangerous Idea*
(Downers Grove, IL: InterVarsity Press, 2003).) Lewis also tackled the issues of
the **problem of evil**, **hell**, and animal suffering in his book, *The Problem
of Pain* (New York: HarperOne, 2001 [1940]).

Mackie, J. L. (1917–81)

J. L. Mackie was one of the 20th century's great philosophical critics of theistic belief. He taught for many years at Oxford University. He may be best known for developing a powerful version of the **logical problem of evil**, but his criticisms of some of the great arguments for God's existence and of belief in **miracles** are also extremely influential and can be found in his classic book *The Miracle of Theism* (London: Oxford, 1982).

Nietzsche, Friedrich (1844–1900)

Nietzsche, the great 19th century German philosopher, was well-known for his pronouncements on the death of God, his criticisms of religion, and his sharply worded calls for people to recognize and live by the implications of **atheism**. He explored the origins of Christianity and of traditional morality, and argued that both represented a clever and successful ploy by the weak to bring the strong down to their level. He preferred a moral code which glorified strength and affirmed life, a code which he believed Christian morality illegitimately supplanted. A brilliant and effective writer, he authored many books; a good place for beginners to start is *A Nietzsche Reader*, R. J. Hollingdale, trans. (New York: Penguin Classics, 1978).

Paley, William (1743–1805)

William Paley was a British philosopher and Christian apologist best known for propounding versions of the **teleological argument** for God's existence. In his book *Natural Theology* (1802), he pointed out that if you found a watch lying on the ground and noted the ways in which its parts work together to fulfill a function, you would conclude it was designed; and he argued that we should conclude the same about the natural world on the basis of observation of earthly creatures and their parts (especially their eyes). While the **theory of evolution** did a fair amount to undercut the force of Paley's argument by offering an explanation of how creatures could appear to be designed in the absence of a designer, Paley's argument remains the subject of much debate, and variations on it have been picked up by the **intelligent design** movement.

Plantinga, Alvin (b. 1932)

Alvin Plantinga is an important contemporary philosopher, one who deserves much credit for the revival of interest in philosophy of religion that took place in the Western academic world in the second half of the 20th century. A Christian who taught for years at Calvin College (Grand Rapids, Michigan) and the University of Notre Dame, Plantinga has had a voice in a number of debates covered in this book. He developed a version of the **ontological argument**, came up with the **free will defense** (and in doing so inadvertently reinvented the theory of **divine providence** known as **Molinism**), and crafted the **evolutionary argument against naturalism**. Perhaps his impact has been felt most strongly in the debate over **evidentialism**, which claims that evidence is required for rational religious belief. In response, Plantinga developed **Reformed epistemology**, rejecting evidentialism and the classical foundationalism on which he took it to be based. His impact on contemporary philosophy of religion has been profound. His books are not easy going for less-experienced readers, but those who enjoy a rewarding challenge are encouraged to try ***God and Other Minds***, *God, Freedom, and Evil* (Grand Rapids: Eerdmans, 1977), and ***Warranted Christian Belief***. See also a collection of his essays, *The Analytic Theist: An Alvin Plantinga Reader*, James F. Sennett, ed. (Grand Rapids: Eerdmans, 1998).

Plato (427–347 B.C.E.)

Plato is a giant of Western philosophy, a philosopher who had something important to say about nearly every topic of philosophical interest. He wrote in dialogue form, with his teacher Socrates (469–399 B.C.E.) serving as the character in the dialogues who usually expresses Plato's own view and usually wins the arguments. Plato's influence in philosophy of religion is difficult to overstate. He is responsible for raising the **Euthyphro problem**, which questions the relation of God to morality. He defended substance **dualism** and the **immortality** of the soul. Much early Christian theology, including the view of God as perfect, outside of time, unchanging, and beyond emotion, can be traced back to Plato and his followers. Many of Plato's dialogues are valuable reading, but *Euthyphro*, **Phaedo**, *Apology*, and *Republic* are essential.

Russell, Bertrand (1872–1970)

Bertrand Russell, a British philosopher and **atheist**, was one of the few 20th century philosophers who achieved significant fame beyond the academic community. He did not write widely in philosophy of religion, but two of his essays are notable: "Why I am not a Christian," which attempts to debunk some of the arguments for God's existence and calls into question the notion of **hell**; and "A Free Man's Worship," an inspiring call to moral behavior on the part of those who believe that there is no God to supply purpose to the world. Both papers can be found in *Why I am not a Christian and Other Essays on Religion and Related Subjects* (New York: George Allen and Unwin Ltd., 1957).

Swinburne, Richard (b. 1934)

The preeminent Christian **evidentialist** and **apologist** of recent years, Swinburne spent most of his career teaching at Oxford University. In his writings he has defended Christian belief on nearly every front. He has explored the major arguments for God's existence, and is well-known for developing a *cumulative case* argument which claims that all things considered (all the evidence for and against God's existence, taken together) it is probable that God exists. He has argued similarly in favor of specifically Christian belief, making the case that the evidence supports the story of Jesus' resurrection, and that the occurrence of this event in turn supports other central claims in Christian theology. He has developed sophisticated arguments for substance **dualism**, and has also more recently sought to provide a plausible explanation of why God allows evil. Particularly notable among his many books are **The Existence of God** 2nd ed. (New York: Oxford University Press, 2004), and *The Coherence of Theism* rev. ed. (New York: Oxford University Press, 1993).

Teresa of Avila (1515–82)

St. Teresa of Avila was a Spanish nun well-known for her mystical experiences, particularly her visions of Jesus. In philosophy of religion, she is often cited in discussions of **religious experience**, since her visions were well-documented and powerfully described. At times in her life, people claimed that her visions were deceptive and were in fact from the devil; but she defended herself by arguing that the positive consequences of the visions and their transforming power in her own life were good evidence that the experiences were authentic. Her autobiography, which recounts her life and visions, is called *The Life of St. Teresa of Avila*, J. M. Cohen, trans. (New York: Penguin, 1957).

Tertullian (ca. 160–ca. 220)

Tertullian, an early Christian theologian, is best known for asking the rhetorical question, "What has Athens to do with Jerusalem?" In other words, what does Greek philosophy have to do with the Christian faith? His apparent answer to the question is, "Nothing." This view came to represent the notion that faith cannot be judged or evaluated by reason, a version of **fideism** that is popular in some circles but a definite minority position in the Christian tradition. It is unlikely that Tertullian himself endorsed the extreme sort of opposition to reason and philosophy that is sometimes ascribed to him, since he was well-versed in Greek philosophy and employed arguments to establish his conclusions. But he was opposed to philosophical views, inspired by **Plato** (427–347 B.C.E.), which chafed at the possibility that the immaterial God might enter the physical world, since Christians believe that God actually did that in the person of Jesus Christ.

Key Texts in Philosophy of Religion

In this chapter we'll note and briefly summarize several important texts in philosophy of religion. The entries in this chapter are chosen on account of their importance and influence in the field and also because they constitute fertile grounds for further study. (Note that many other important texts and articles are cited, sometimes with main arguments summarized, in the previous two chapters of this book.) Entries are listed alphabetically by author. When bibliographical information is not given, that means that the texts are available from many publishers and possibly on the internet as well.

Anselm, *Proslogium*. This short work by St. Anselm (1033–1109) exemplifies his approach of "faith seeking understanding." In his introduction he reveals that he is attempting to use reason to comprehend what he already believes by faith about the existence and nature of God. In the first three chapters, two influential versions of the **ontological argument** for God's existence are proposed; Anselm argues that we cannot even conceive of God not existing, since any being that we can conceive of not existing is not as great as God. In subsequent chapters Anselm dwells on some of the attributes of God, particularly God's timelessness, justice, and compassion—the last presenting a puzzle since, on the medieval view endorsed by Anselm, God feels no emotion. In addition, Anselm ponders the nature of God's **omnipotence**, and contends that the fact that God is incapable of doing wrong is not a problem for omnipotence, since the ability to do wrong is not a power but an "impotence," and hence one who lacks that ability is more powerful for it.

Aquinas, *Summa Contra Gentiles* and *Summa Theologica*. These two works by Thomas Aquinas (1225–74) pull together his views on the nature of God, the relation of faith and reason, and on nearly all matters of Christian theology. Here we cannot summarize much of them except to note their basic structure and highlight where he deals with some of the terms and concepts already discussed in this book.

The *Summa Contra Gentiles* (which means "Summary against the Gentiles") was written first, and finished in 1264. It contains four books. Book I is probably of most interest to introductory readers in philosophy of religion, since it contains Aquinas's views on faith and reason, his arguments for God's existence, and his reflections on God's attributes (which includes his explication of the theory of **analogy**, which specifies how our concepts apply to God). Book II includes Aquinas's discussion of creation (a point on which he disagreed with **Aristotle** (384–322 B.C.E.) who believed that the world was not created), and his account of human beings, an account that seems to be something of a blend between substance **dualism** and **materialism**. In Book III, Aquinas turns to human happiness, our end or purpose, which he contends consists finally in the contemplation of God. In Book IV he discusses some of the niceties of Christian doctrine, exploring revealed truth rather than truth that can be discovered by reason.

The *Summa Theologica* covers some of the same ground, often in more detail. Aquinas died before completing it, but the book is still massive. (In the Prologue Aquinas expresses his desire to "propound the things belonging to the Christian religion in a way consonant with the instruction of beginners." On that point he may not have succeeded!) Aquinas writes systematically, and his discussion has the following structure: he asks a question, proposes a number of answers to it that differ from his own, then gives his own, and then concludes the section by explaining the errors of the other answers. A number of characters continually show up in the discussion, including **Augustine** (354–430) and Aristotle, whom he calls the Theologian and the Philosopher respectively.

The work is divided into three major parts, with the second part being itself divided in two. (References to the *Summa Theologica* in other writings cite it by numbers, such as, for his discussion of the theory of analogy, 1. 13. 5, meaning that that discussion takes place in the first part, thirteenth question, fifth article.) The first part of the book includes discussions of the existence and nature of God, and the nature of human beings. The second part talks again about human happiness (our end or function), virtues and vices, and about **natural law** and its relation to human law. The third part of the book deals more specifically with matters of faith—the incarnation, for instance, and the sacraments.

Aquinas's *Summas* can be read in their entirety, but abridged editions and excerpts from both books (for example, the treatises on the divine nature, on law, on happiness, and on human nature) are widely available in print and on the internet.

Augustine, *Confessions of Saint Augustine*. This book, Augustine's (354–430) autobiography, written c. 400, has been read for centuries largely because of its honest early portrayal of a man on a religious quest that ultimately leads him to Christianity. In it Augustine describes his youthful struggles with sinful behavior (including the well-known episode where he steals some pears just for the joy of doing what was forbidden), and his dramatic conversion. Most significant for philosophy of religion are his reflections on the **problem of evil**, which initially steered him to a version of cosmic **dualism** (Manichaeism) but eventually made him open to Christianity when he concluded that evil was the absence of good and hence not something that God created. The final chapters of the book also include a discussion of the nature of time.

Boethius, *Consolation of Philosophy*. Boethius (ca. 480–525) was a Roman scholar and civil servant who wrote this important little book near the end of his life, when he was imprisoned and in desperate straits. In the book he attempts through a discussion between himself and "Lady Philosophy" to come to grips with the tension between the misery of his own circumstances and the providence of a loving God. Following the ancient Greeks and **Augustine** (354–430) he affirms that happiness cannot be found in the pursuit of worldly goods but only in the pursuit of the highest good, God. Misfortune may come, as Boethius well knew, but knowledge of God reveals that whatever God does or permits must be good, despite our inability to understand and despite the pain that may result for us. Perhaps the best-known part of the book involves Boethius's attempt, in Book V, to square **divine providence** with human **free will**. For Boethius, the solution to this problem is found in the relation of **God and time**. God, being outside time, does not have foreknowledge, but instead sees all at once; but seeing what we do as we do it does not threaten our ability to act freely.

Descartes, *Meditations on First Philosophy*. This landmark book by René Descartes (1596–1650), has many important implications for philosophy of religion. Divided into six separate meditations, it opens with Descartes setting out to determine what he can know for certain. He has come to many false beliefs in the past, he says, so it's time to start from scratch by eliminating all beliefs about which he might be mistaken and rebuilding his belief system on indubitable foundations. Much of the book constitutes his attempt to do this. At least three important points from philosophy of religion can be found in this discussion. First, we find an inclination toward **evidentialism** in Descartes' contention that since God gave him his cognitive faculties, he has a duty to employ them correctly by believing only what he can clearly see to be true. Second, Descartes claims that he is an immaterial soul, on the grounds that he can imagine himself existing without his body. This argument (and others he gives) for substance **dualism** has been highly influential and reworked recently by **Richard Swinburne** (b. 1934). Third, in the fifth meditation Descartes proposes a version of the **ontological argument** which claims that God, defined as a perfect being, exists by definition, since no being can be perfect which fails to exist.

Hume, David, *Dialogues Concerning Natural Religion*. This book by David Hume (1711–76) was not published until after his death, perhaps because of the sensitivity of the subject matter. The dialogue is (mostly) between three fictional characters: Cleanthes, a proponent of **natural theology**; Demea, a sort of **fideist** who doubts that we can know God's nature through reason; and Philo, a skeptic whose views probably most closely mirror Hume's. Two discussions in the book are particularly noteworthy. The first is of the **teleological argument** which is defended by Cleanthes but attacked by the other two. Cleanthes argues that if we look round the world we should see that it is like a machine, and that just as machines have designers, the world must as well. Philo and Demea criticize the argument and in particular the notion that we can infer anything about the nature of the designer from the nature of the world. A second fascinating discussion has to do with the **problem of evil**. A powerful description of the nature of evil is found in Book X; and Philo (and perhaps Hume) concludes from his experience of the world that the First Cause is most likely indifferent to it, and hence that we cannot infer from what we see that the God of **theism** exists.

James, William, "The Will to Believe". This essay by William James (1842–1910) presents an important response to **evidentialism** and particularly to its outspoken proponent **W. K. Clifford** (1845–79). In it, James argues that under certain conditions it is perfectly acceptable, and even recommended, to believe something without sufficient evidence. When you have a choice between competing hypotheses—that is, between two possible belief options—both of which are "live" (have some plausibility for you), where the choice between them is "forced" (you cannot put it off) and "momentous" (a lot is at stake), and where sufficient evidence is not and will not be available to decide the matter, it is acceptable for you to allow your passions to guide your choice and to believe in the absence of evidence. James uses this reasoning to concoct a pragmatic argument for religious faith, similar to a **pragmatic argument for belief in God**. Religious faith, he says, claims that the best things are eternal and that you are better off now if you believe that. Assuming religion is a live option for you, the option to believe is also momentous, since there is so much at stake in believing, and it is forced in so far as you will lose out if you hold off believing until more evidence comes your way (as evidentialism requires you to do). Thus, if the evidence for and against religion is inconclusive, you can, and should, follow your heart and adopt the will to believe.

Pascal, *Pensees*. This work by Blaise Pascal (1623–62), a brilliant French mathematician and philosopher, is an unpolished but important collection of his "thoughts" on religion. Perhaps best known for its development of **Pascal's Wager**, the book also includes profound reflections on the relation between faith and reason, where Pascal attempts to steer a path between the extremes of **fideism** and **rationalism**. Against rationalism, he warns that "the heart has its reasons of which reason knows nothing," and that submitting everything about religion to reason will strip the mystery and vitality from it. At the same time, against fideism, he contends that an unreasoned faith is bound to be ridiculous. He also speaks critically of philosophical arguments for the existence of God; he thinks that they are successful neither in establishing their conclusion nor in bringing people closer to God.

Plantinga, Alvin, *God and Other Minds* (Ithaca: Cornell, 1967). This early book by Plantinga (b. 1932) was written prior to his rejection of **evidentialism** and is dedicated to investigating arguments for and against God's existence. After considering the great arguments for God's existence and finding them wanting, Plantinga turns to the arguments against God's existence (in particular the **problem of evil**) and pays them the same compliment. He concludes by arguing from **analogy** as follows: while we have no conclusive arguments that other people have minds (we can't see their minds nor experience what they do), we are justified in believing that indeed they do; but since belief in God is similar to belief in other minds, we are likewise justified in believing in God.

Plantinga, Alvin, *Warranted Christian Belief* (New York: Oxford, 2000). In this recent book Plantinga (b. 1932) brings **Reformed epistemology** to its logical conclusion. Here's the background. **Evidentialism** claims that beliefs must be based on evidence in order to be rational or justified. Reformed epistemology denies this and contends that theists can justifiably *start* with belief in God without holding it on the basis of evidence. In *Warranted Christian Belief*, Plantinga expands this position by applying it to central Christian beliefs, like belief in the resurrection and the trinity. He argues that these beliefs can also be justified and rational, and can even amount to knowledge. To support this contention, Plantinga spends considerable time exploring what is required for knowing something. Drawing on his earlier writings in **epistemology**, Plantinga argues that whether a true belief amounts to knowledge depends on whether it is produced in us by properly functioning cognitive faculties (under those conditions, the belief has *warrant*). If the Christian story is true and God tells us that it is, then belief in the story meets those conditions and hence amounts to knowledge. Notice Plantinga's conditional conclusion: *if* Christian belief is true, *then* it amounts to knowledge. But is it true? Plantinga argues that we cannot prove that it is; but since evidentialism is false, our inability to prove by evidence the truth of our beliefs does not prevent those beliefs from being rational, justified, and known.

Plato, *Phaedo*. This dialogue by Plato (427–347 B.C.E.) has Socrates (469–399 B.C.E.) in prison discussing his impending execution with some young friends. (Socrates drinks hemlock and dies at the end of the dialogue.) The dialogue includes arguments for two conclusions important in philosophy of religion: first, substance **dualism**, the thesis that a person is an immaterial soul housed in a material body; and second, the **immortality** of the soul. Several arguments for both are given. For example, in favor of dualism Plato (using Socrates as his voice) argues that the mind can reason without input from the body and hence must be separate from it; and for immortality he argues that the soul's desire for the truth is hindered by the body, and this desire must be fulfilled after death when the soul is freed from it. Hence, as Socrates says, true philosophers look forward to death, when they will be released from their bodies and left free to acquire the wisdom that they seek, in the realm of what is divine, changeless, and eternal.

Swinburne, Richard, *The Existence of God* 2nd ed. (New York: Oxford University Press, 2004). This book is a classic defense of belief in God from the challenge to it posed by **evidentialism**. In the book, Swinburne (b. 1934) treats God's existence as a hypothesis to be rendered probable or improbable by the evidence, and he offers a cumulative case argument that it is more likely than not that God does exist. After explaining that the theistic hypothesis is an initially appealing one in so far as the existence of an infinite, **omnipotent**, **omniscient** being could serve as an ultimate explanation for everything else there is, he turns to the classic arguments for God's existence, particularly the **cosmological** and **teleological arguments**. He also provides arguments for God's existence from **miracle** reports and from **religious experience**. Each argument by itself, he concedes, does not render the theistic hypothesis more probable than not, but taken altogether they do (and this is so even when the **problem of evil** is factored into the equation). Thus his conclusion is that it is more likely than not that God exists.

Index

Note: Numbers in **bold** indicate the page(s) where the term, thinker, or text has its own entry.